Diving & S

GUAM

and the Mariana Islands

By TIM ROCK

Cetti Bay, Guam

Guam manta ray

About the Author:

Tim Rock is an internationally published photojournalist who specializes in the ocean realm. Based on Guam in the Western Pacific Ocean, Rock has traveled Micronesia, the Indo-Pacific and worldwide for three decades. He is the author of numerous Lonely Planet Diving & Snorkeling guides, produced the ACE award finalist Aquaquest Micronesia Television series and has won awards from the AP, UPI and NPPA for writing and photography. His website: www.doubleblue.com

Acknowledgements

A special thanks to MDA owner Lee Webber on Guam who encouraged me to publish my first guide a couple of decades ago. Pete and Linda Peterson and Jim Miller, who have been strong supporters of many of my personal projects over the years. Thanks to Mark and Lynn Michael of Rota who have been good for diving and good for Rota. Also thanks to Sam Marcos and Rick Northen on Saipan.

Photographic Equipment Used

Rock uses Aquatica underwater housings with Ikelite strobes and TLC arms. He uses Nikon cameras with Nikon, Sigma and Tokina lenses.

Main Modeling by Elaine Kwok. Additional modeling by Ai Futaki, Stefanie Brendl, Simon Pridmore, Bill Cooper and Lori Mendiola.
In memory of Kumiko Furukawa.

ISBN # 978-0-9838962-2-7

Agat Marina

Diving & Snorkeling Guide to

GUAM

and the Mariana Islands

CONTENTS:

Guam's Tumon Bay

Umatac Bay overlook

How to Use This Guide

This guide is intended to bring to the diver the most popular and unique dive sites of the Mariana Islands. Guam, Rota and Saipan are places known for their wide array of beautiful hard corals, variety of fish and other marine life and plethora of invertebrates. Approximate dive positions are shown on the maps and each site is introduced with general location, most frequently dived depths, and type of dive that can be expected, the dominant marine life and the logistical requirements.

Guam has a population of about 170,000 people, many of whom are transient and learn scuba while living on the island. Guam is a very popular dive destination for the Japanese tourist and is gaining in popularity with other Asian travellers. It has a great variety of sites. This book has the best snorkeling reefs, beach dives, shipwrecks and the popular boat dives.

Rota is a unique departure for the diver. This pristine little isle offers a great variety of diving as well in exceptionally clear water.

Saipan is the capitol of the Northern

Fish Eye Marine Park dancers

Mariana Islands. Walls, caves, coral gardens and a resident population of easily observed eagle rays give Saipan its claim to fame. Saipan dives can be done with a boat and local guide and a few are walk-ins, like the famous Grotto.

There are, of course, numerous dive sites at each island. This is not intended to be a complete travel guide, but a clear overview of the dive potential at each locale, with emphasis on the larger and more populous Guam.

The waters of these islands generally have incredible water clarity and the water is considered to be warm in comparison to most international locales. Be alert for changing conditions and, because the clarity can be deceptive, monitor depth closely.

Before making any dive consider the way you feel that particular day, your level of training, physical condition and water conditions at the site. It is no sin to abort a dive. Remember the old adage: "There are old divers and there are bold divers but there aren't many old, bold divers."

Be honest in evaluating your diving skills.

Rota taga stone quarry

Overview

The undersea terrain of Guam, Rota and Saipan is not known for its sea fans and soft corals as are the reefs and shipwrecks of popular island neighbors like Truk and Palau. But these islands can be aptly described as hard coral kingdoms. Some 400 species of coral and over 900 species of fish inhabit these incredible reefs. There is much diversity and intense growth competition on the healthy reefs.

Fish and invertebrates use the nooks, crannies and other protective spaces as homes and refuges. A great variety of fish, many in colorful juvenile stages, will be easily found by diving casually and looking closely. The corals also provide home for a broad range of anemones. Some are shaped like small door mats with resident glass shrimp and colorful polyps adorning the outer edges. Others are broad carpets with flowing tentacles and hosts of bright clownfish.

Piti Bomb Holes

The islands do have undersea dropoffs holding fans and soft corals. Guam's Hospital Point and Orote Peninsula, sheer, blue and deep, are practically unrivalled for water clarity. And Rota's caves and points are breathtaking. Rota is said to have the clearest waters in the Pacific.

This region is blessed with a great variety of fish life. It is not unusual to see dolphins, reef sharks, barracuda schools, manta rays, parrotfish, Napoleon wrasse, crevalle jacks, eagle rays, groupers and reef tropicals during the course of a week's diving. Even sperm whales have been sighted.

Guam's Sella Bay

Overview: GUAM

Guam is a melting pot of Micronesian, Carolinian and Asian cultures. A drive around the island may get you caught in a traffic jam on a six-lane highway at rush hour. All of the popular fast and chain food restaurants are here and movie complexes with all the current hits are in the big malls.

But, A half hour later, you can be rolling down a traffic-free road enjoying scenic hills and valleys covered with coconut palms and flowing swordgrasses.

You may have to brake for a boy riding a caraboa down a quiet village street and the only things lining the road are quaint, colorful houses adorned with bright, tropical flowers.

Many people in the military feel Guam is one of the best duty stations offered, but Guam actually has a large civilian population of around 150,000. A major player in the Asian tourism market, it is the "Caribbean of Japan", attracting over a million (mostly Japanese) visitors annually.

Guam is superb for those who love the sea and the outdoors. Not only does Guam have a lush tropical atmosphere, but the central business district is a bustling area offering all of the amenities found stateside while its agricultural areas in the north and south feature historic villages nestled in the quiet hills and valleys

Guam's first inhabitants are believed to have come to Guam about 2000 years before Christ and may have been Malaysian. Natives of Guam are called Chamorros and the present native population are direct descendents of these people although their bloodlines have been mixed over decades of Spanish, American and brief Japanese rule. The island also boasts a large Filipino population spanning many generations.

Today's Chamorros are a progressive lot who have long left their subsistence existence behind.

Bougainvillea

Guamanians are U.S. citizens and pay taxes. The first governor was elected in 1970. Guam has a 15-seat unicameral legislature. English and Chamorro are the official languages and English is spoken by all. The Filipino, Japanese, Chinese, Korean and Micronesian communities are also strongly represented on Guam.

For visitors, Guam has a well-staffed entity, The Guam Visitor's Bureau or GVB. It can be contacted at 671-646-5278. The GVB website is: www.visitguam.org.

Geography

Guam is the southernmost island in the Mariana chain, 30 miles long and nine miles at its widest. Not large by most standards, but it is the largest island in Micronesia. The north comprises raised limestone plateau. The south is a mix of high volcanic hills and valleys with rivers and falls spilling to the sea. In the south is a barrier reef with an adjoining island.

Guam is the tip of possibly the highest mountain in the world. The Marianas Trench, the world's deepest ocean site, lies just southeast of Guam. The undersea terrain features mainly sloping reefs. The southwest features a broad bay. Steep walls along the clifflines and outer reef slopes fall quickly into a blue abyss. The protected harbor is full of patch reefs and shipwrecks and is diveable pretty much year 'round.

Climate

Guam's climate is uniformly warm and humid. Evening temps average 74F (23C) and 88F (32C) during the day. Cooler trade wind season runs from late December to May. June through September features calm seas and little breeze with scattered daily showers. Stronger rains are usually in October and November. Guam lies in the typhoon belt and big storms can come in the last half of the year.

The windward or eastern side of Guam is most accessible during the summer months as are the far offshore reefs. Then, the seas are normally glassy calm and flat.

The western side of the island, especially the Agat Bay and points south, is normally protected most of the year and good for diving.

Visibility is affected by runoff, so rainy season months mean lower visibility. Tides do not vary greatly on Guam but visibility is best at high morning incoming tide. Currents do not affect most dive sites, but can be strong along

Wild caraboa, central Guam

the deep outer reef sites.

Water here is tropical (average about 80 degrees) and only a dive-skin is normally necessary for warmth and protection from abrasions or stings.

Getting There:

Getting to Guam is not a problem. Guam is served daily by major carriers from all over the Asian region and from the U.S. through Honolulu. Guam's main carrier is United Continental Micronesia. International airline carriers service Guam's $50 million air terminal with connections to most major cities. Domestic airlines also service the neighboring islands.

Getting Around:

Taxis can be expensive on Guam. It is best to rent a car while visiting. All of the major rental agencies are here. Micronesia Divers Association has a hotel/dive package. Do not depend on the public bus system to go far afield. The Tumon shopping buses run on time.

Entry

A valid US passport is required to enter Guam, even for US citizens. US citizens can stay as long as they want. All non-US citizens require a US visa to visit Guam. There is a liberal visa waiver program that allows for up to 15-day (only) stays.

Check with the Guam Visitor's Bureau's website at www.visitguam.org to see if your country participates.

Currency

The US dollar is the accepted rate of currency. All major credit cards are accepted most everywhere for virtually everything. Money exchange can be found on Tumon Bay and at the Guam airport.

WWII gun, Gun Beach

Time

Guam is located on the western side of the international dateline. Coming from Hawaii or points east you lose a day when crossing the international dateline. Guam is 10 hours ahead of GMT/UTC. When its noon on Guam, Saipan and Rota it is 6 pm the day before in San Francisco.

Electricity

Electricity is 110/120 volts, 60 cycle and the flat, two-pronged plug is used, same as in the USA. Some major hardware stores sell adapters for 220V but it is best to bring one with you if you need it.

Weights & Measures

The imperial system of measurement is used. Distances: inches, feet, yards, miles. Weights: ounces, pounds, tons. Air on scuba gauges is read in pounds and underwater depth is read in feet.

WHAT TO BRING

Hawksbill sea turtle

General Supplies

You can get anything on Guam as far as basic living goes. Prices are similar to those in Hawaii. Lightweight clothing is available at all clothing stores. Bring only necessities like prescription medicines and items very specific to your lifestyle.

What to Wear

Dress is normally casual and islandwear is always acceptable, whatever the occasion. Light summer clothing is appropriate, however, keep in mind that the chill of an air-conditioned interior may require a light sweater.

On the dive boat, the sun is hot and water reflective. Bring high factor suntan spray, a hat and perhaps a long-sleeved T-shirt. A light rain poncho is handy to protect against the chill of showers and fits handily into a dive bag.

Dive Related Equipment

Guam is well-stocked for equipment and offers fine repair facilities. Rota and Saipan also keep some rental supply on hand. Guam is well-known for bargain prices. MDA (Micronesia Diver's Association) is a major regional wholesaler and has some quality sales.

There is a wide range of equipment and brands of equipment for sale on the island. Water here is warm and dive skins and thin wetsuits are used mostly for protection from sunburn, coral cuts, stings and other minor marine hazards.

Underwater Photography

Guam does not have a major professionally stocked camera store. There are some discount houses like Cost-U-Less and K-Mart that have batteries and some camera SD and Flash cards. If you are in the military, the exchanges carry some higher end, though not pro, DSLR cameras and lenses.

Underwater photographers should bring their own gear and back-ups if visiting. Housing sales and stock are limited. Marine Images in Fish Eye is an Aquatica and Ikelite dealer and MDA next door also carries Ikelite and some other housings.

Housings for point-and-shoot cameras are available in some stores and MDA

offers package deals to include strobes.

Some styles of video cameras, especially JVC, Sony and Canon, are available at the local dealer.

Business Hours/Holidays

Most businesses are open 10 to 7 and many are open until 10 pm. Bars are open until 1 or 2 am on weekdays and weekends.

Accommodations

Luxurious international-standard hotels are set in landscaped gardens on the beaches of Tumon Bay, the island's premier resort destination.

A few hotels are also located in the southern and central parts of the island. A number of fine business hotels and family style accommodations are located in Hagatña, Maite, Tumon, Tamuning and just minutes away from the A.B. Won Pat Guam International Air Terminal.

Although scuba diving, especially intro dives for Japanese tourists, is popular, there aren't many that offer dive/hotel packages for the experienced travelling diver. But there are many "name brand" hotels here and online reservations are easily made. There is a hotel tax of about 10 percent.

Tipping

Tipping is an accepted practice. Some hotels and restaurants add a 10 percent service charge to the restaurant bill, so additional tipping is optional. The standard rate for restaurant service, taxi drivers, and hotel service personnel is 10 to 15 percent.

Dining/Food

Guam is a haven of the culinary arts. As Guam is such a great melting pot, a wide array of fine restaurants offer delicacies to please any palate. Major hotels and restaurants serve high-quality Continental meals; many offer exotic ethnic dishes, as well.

There is a bountiful variety of fresh seafood, although little of it is caught on Guam. Fresh fish, octopus, and lobster are served either grilled or baked with vegetables or fruit, sashimi (raw fish), and in other imaginative ways unique to the Pacific.

Travelers who venture further into Guam will find Chamorro, Japanese, Korean, Thai, Vietnamese, Filipino, Chinese, Mexican, and European eating establishments. Each has its own charm and ambiance. Of course, American fast food chains have become standard fare for those on the go. Try Chamorro Village on Wednesday nights for great food at the Night Market.

Shopping

Shopping on Guam can provide the opportunity to decorate your home and enlarge your wardrobe with some of the finest purchases to be found in this part of the Pacific Rim.

In the way of buys for the home, there is an opportunity to pick up some of the best and most unique art pieces in the world. The islanders of the western Pacific are known for their handiwork. Pohnpei is famous for its carving of sharks, dolphins and other sea creatures made from mangrove wood. The Marshall islands offer some of the most intricate and unique weavings in the world. Truk is famous for its carved heads and the ever popular love sticks. And visit in Micronesia isn't complete without obtaining a storyboard from the Republic of Palau. Guam has some amazing necklaces and carvings.

Try Guam's Chamorro Village shopping center for an array of ethnic arts. Crafts and great T-shirts can be found at Fish Eye in Piti. The Micronesia Mall brings more trendy fare and Guam's Tumon Bay is loaded with duty free and designer labels.

Illegal Items

Guam laws basically mirror all California state laws and all federal laws. Tobacco and alcohol are the only legal drugs. Importation and possession of turtle shell and other endangered species items is also illegal.

Customs checks are performed upon entry to Guam. Visitors are allowed to bring three cartons of cigarettes, three bottles of spirits, and reasonable amounts of perfume for personal use into duty free Guam. Plants, fruits and veggies are forbidden due to insects they might introduce.

Balloons, Asan park

undeveloped southern coastline provide a nice look at Guam's geologic, historic and natural history. The Talofofo River is developed minimally for tourism and river boat tours run past large stands of bamboo and lead to a restored latte site. This can also be done by kayak.

Guam's wildlife is not easily observable as most of it resides on restricted military areas. The brown tree snake, an introduced pest, has been responsible for the loss of land snails that has meant a loss of food for wild birds. The snake also eats birds and Guam's bird population is quite low but getting stronger in some places.

Guam does have a herd of wild caraboa. Monitor lizards, wild pigs, wild deer, abundant geckoes and toads and the banana spider are all found on the island.

Activities and Attractions

Guam attracts over a million tourists annually. It is kind of like summer all year round. Snorkeling, swimming, trolling, scuba diving, kite surfing, wind surfing, sailing, sky diving and parasailing top the things to do. Guam has running clubs, biking and hiking clubs and all sorts of outdoor groups with whom one can enjoy the tropics. Guam has many 18-hole golf courses.

All types of watersports, tours and night activities can be found. For the nature lover, hikes into Guam's jungles can be fun. There are organized Saturday hikes and nothing in the way of plant or animal life is dangerous. Sea kayaking is becoming popular and tours and trips along Guam's largely

Southern coast kayaking

Sea turtle with remora

Boat Diving

Most tourist divers to Guam will want to visit the World War II shipwrecks and the novelty dives like the Blue Hole or the Crevice, which are known for their water clarity. Daily charters to the popular sites are available through the local dive shops.

Boat diving is probably the safest way to approach the reefs and there is a higher likelihood of seeing fish and other sea creatures at the popular sites, where some fish feeding has become a practice.

The surf on Guam can be tricky and unpredictable. Those used to a surf entry in, say, California, could be in for a rude surprise on Guam as the water crosses a broad reef flat before breaking. Undercurrents and rips in the cuts are strong when the surf is up. The safety rule of thumb is to use a boat if the surf isn't slapping your ankles .

The harbor dives are all on hard coral reefs or shipwrecks and can be quite nice. Most of them are just a short ride from the docks and the harbor is well-protected, so dives can be made there pretty much year 'round.

Many reefs cascade down gently sloping to 90 feet or deeper. The shipwrecks range in the 60 to 120 foot category.

The outer reefs provide a variety ranging from deep dropoffs to ranging coral flats. Guam has had a siltation problem on its reefs due to rapid development, but many of the offshore reefs have escaped this blight and are homes to a wide variety of fish, sea anemones and hard and soft corals.

Boat dives during the week cater mainly to Japanese tourists, so Guam diving can easily become a cross-cultural experience as well. There are a

Divers in Piti Bay

number of divemasters and instructors who work through the local shops to provide service on a one-to-one basis by using their private boats. If you have specific sites in mind or want to keep your group small, ask the local shops about a private charter.

The larger charter boats also offer early morning single tank dives and afternoon/evening dives that include on deck bar-b-queues and a night dive.

Night diving on Guam is very good as a lot of unusual invertebrates hide in the hard corals during the day and come out at night. Ask about the availability of these dives.

Instruction

All levels of instruction are available on Guam from snorkeling and basic open water to instructorship. Technical diving to the instructor level is also taught here. PADI is the major training organization represented here, but there are others as well.

Guam's unique terrain and various walls, wrecks, caves and dropoffs is perfect for learning all kinds of advanced techniques.

Pre-trip Preps

As far as diving equipment goes, you can show up with nothing and leave with just about every gadget known to diving. Guam has a very active local diving population and many stores are fully stocked with the top brand names at very competitive pricing. However, most travelling divers are very comfortable with their own gear, so bring your own gear and add toys. Camera equipment and film are available but not in the abundance of dive gear. Bring what you need for still and video work (see previous section).

Medical

Guam has two fully-staffed recompression chambers run by the US Navy and two hospitals, one military and one civilian. It has physicians highly trained in diving accidents and medicine. It is recommended that all divers hold DAN or similar comprehensive diving insurance.

Guam Memorial Hospital, 850 Gov. Carlos Camacho Rd. Tamuning, GU 96911, Tel: (671) 647-2330

Spinner dolphins, Agat Bay

Blue chromis

Guam Snorkeling

Manta ray

For those who may not have the time or training to do a lot of diving but still want to see what the sea life is like, snorkeling and marine destinations abound. This is also great family fun. For example, Guam has five zoned areas as marine preserves. One of these is Fish Eye Marine Park/Piti Bomb Holes. Here you can snorkel on your own or join a Fish Eye tour and visit an undersea observatory.

This walk-in site has more than 200 fish species as it is a marine preserve and incubator for fish and invertebrates. You can see the healthy reef on the south side of the observatory, feed the fish and even snorkel around the observatory itself. A visit to the unique observatory is also included in the guided tour.

The guided tour has seven stops and looks at various fish life, different kinds of corals and also a sea anemone colony with clownfish.

Afterwards, take a trip inside the observatory, have lunch and visit the gift shop in the Fish Eye facility across the street. There is also the free Tim Rock undersea marine photography gallery found here.

Another easy walk-in snorkel is at one of Guam's favorite beach parks in Tumon Bay. Ypao Beach Park sits on the Tumon Bay Marine Preserve. It has clear waters and brilliant white sand, so it is a great place to enjoy the many corals and fishes. Palm trees and picnic tables are found beachside so one can have lunch before or after the snorkel. Also, there is normally a lifeguard on duty.

There is an inshore current here and if the current is strong, the snorkeler can do a drift along the reeftop and just walk back up the beach when finished with this free ride from Nature.

You can do these on your own or as part of a snorkel tour package. Doing both is a full day of enjoying the wonderful marine life of the Pacific.

Guam has many shallow walk-in sites so those who enjoy snorkeling can explore inside the barrier reef all around the island given proper sea and wave conditions.

Southern Dive sites

1) Blue Hole
2) Barracuda Rock
3) The Crevice
4) Shark Pit
5) Eel Gardens
6) Rizal Coral Heads
7) Hap's Reef
8) Gaan Point & The Amtrac
9) Coral Gardens
10) Pete's Reef
11) Agat Bay
12) Nathan's Dent
13) Fouha Bay
14) Toguan Bay
15) Cocos Wall
16) Cocos Island Lagoon

Central & Northern Dives

17) Piti Channel
18) Piti Bomb Holes
19) Asan Cut and Beach
20) Hospital Point
21) Tumon Bay / Ypao Beach
22) Gun Beach
23) Double Reef
24) Pati Point Preserve

Blue Hole

1) Blue Hole

Location: Orote Peninsula
Attractions: Cavern, Sea whips, Fish
Depth: 60 to 130 feet
Logistics: Boat Dive

Guam's Blue Hole is one of the island's finest variety dives. Located toward the tip of the Orote Peninsula on the southern coast, the hole can usually be seen from the surface directly in front of the A-marker. It is a popular spot and has been the site of everything from movie making to weddings and military re-enlistments.

It is basically a long, perpendicular shaft that starts at the top of a sloping reef flat in about 60 feet of water. The shaft itself extends down to about 300 feet, but at 130 feet a large window opens to the outer wall, allowing the diver to exit and ascend after a free fall through the shaft.

As the Blue Hole faces the open ocean, it is not unusual to see large fish out in the blue like dogtooth tuna. Eagle rays have been seen gliding along the reef top and, on rare occasions, even whale sharks. Pilot whales have joined boats traveling to the hole.

Another nice thing about diving here, the Blue Hole is located away from runoff areas and visibility here normally exceeds 100 feet. A Blue Hole dive needs to be well-planned as it is on the deeper spectrum of sport diving. The top of the hole is at 60 feet and once over the edge, the free fall begins. Many divers like to assume the role of skydiver and slowly drift down through the window. This is indeed fun, but there are things to see along the way.

At 80 feet, there is a large crevice that is home to many soldierfish. They

Blue Hole

orient themselves to the bottom and many swim upside down in the recesses of the hole.

At 100 feet there are a few crimson sea whips along the northern wall that make for colorful photographs. At this depth, they look brown but are red if lit up by a light or photographed with a strobe. Outside the wall, look for square spot and golden anthias. They are usually around 100 feet or deeper and move quickly, so they make beautiful but challenging photo subjects.

After the deep part of the dive, swim west and look for resting sea turtles at the rocks. Lionfish and other tropicals also stay here.

At night, the rare flashlight fish comes out. It biochemically illuminates a sac under its eyes and sends flickers of light into the black water. When active, the school resembles fireflies with their flashing lights. Look for them inside the hole at 100 feet.

2) Barracuda Rock

Location: Orote Peninsula
Attractions: Cave, Boulders, and Fish
Depth: 15 to 60 feet
Logistics: Boat Dive

This is a good spot for a shallow second dive. It is a fun place to poke around the small cliffline cave and the tunnel through the big boulders.

Bubble rings

Tangs and surgeonfish

The Dolphins

Guam's coastal waters are the home of pods of dolphins called spinners who use the island's shallow bays for a number of reasons. A very few lucky locals have even established a rapport with the animals and have had regular snorkeling sessions with them in the Merizo end of the island.

The spinner dolphins cruise at speeds between 5 to 7 miles an hour, with a maximum speed of up to 22 mph. So, if you are diving or snorkeling and the dolphins slow down long enough to play with you, it is because they want to. Spinners are normally quite shy and don't play like the bigger bottlenose dolphins.

It is this fact, among others, that makes a dolphin encounter on Guam a special experience. What they do do is leap from the water, spinning and doing amazing acrobatic tricks. They will also surf the stern wake of a boat or ride the bow wave.

There are no trained dolphins on Guam to swim with. All dolphin encounters are in-the-wild happenings. Pacific spinner dolphins (Stinella longirostris) come in to Guam's calm bays and rest by day then leave at night to hunt.

They are easily identified as they have slender bodies and a long thin snout or beak. The flippers and flukes are large and pointed and they are medium-to-dark gray on their topsides and the underbelly is quite pale.

The larger dolphins reach a size of 7 feet in length and weigh up to 200 pounds. They are known to live for 25 to 30 years.

Spinner dolphins

Christmas tree worm

A colony of noddies occupies the big rock that marks this site. They will fly over approaching boats at first, but then settle down almost camouflaged on the volcanic boulder.

There is a small cave in the Orote cliffline that is home to a school of glassy copper sweepers. The cave isn't deep, nor does it go back very far, but there are stalactites that hang down, so be careful not to hit your head, especially if free diving inside the cave.

Outside the cave, to the right as you face the cliffline, is a tunnel that also has sweepers and bigeyes hiding in its recesses. Other fish swim through here and turtles have been known to sleep here at night.

The big boulders in the very clear 30 to 60 foot water are home for a variety of different fish from juvenile Napoleon wrasse to regal angelfish. At night, the nocturnal fish, like lionfish, are joined by starfish, crabs and invertebrates .

3) The Crevice

Location: Orote Peninsula
Attractions: Dropoff, Sea Fans, Fish
Depth: 60 to 130 feet
Logistics: Boat Dive

This deep dive along the Orote Peninsula is pretty but not overly endowed with marine life. There are golden gorgonian fans deep into the crevice and some soft corals. Lace corals fill some of the smaller fissures here. The thrill of this dive is that at times some big creature from the open sea might appear. Sailfish and whale sharks have been reported as have eagle rays and mantas. But they are not frequently encountered.

Deep at the Crevice's bottom, sleeping sharks can be occasionally seen from above. The bottom is beyond safe sport diving limits but it is a rush to look down there and beyond. Properly

The unusual Eel Goby

Shark Pit amtrac

outfitted techies do go there.

The outer wall can also provide some surprises and people like to do drift dives from the Crevice to the Blue Hole when the currents are right.

The upper sand flats of the Crevice have been selected as decompression stop areas, although none of the reeftop gives a really shallow spot for divers to stop. But fish feeding has made many fish approachable including goatfish, parrotfish and pyramids.

Decompression stops should be taken on the mooring buoy lines that are situated at the Crevice.

4) The Shark Pit

Location: Orote Peninsula
Attractions: Large Rock, Military Dumpsite and Fish
Depth: 15 to 130 feet
Logistics: Boat Dive

A huge rock rises to within 15 feet of the surface at the Shark Pit and then tapers down. The bottom recesses have cracks with golden gorgonian sea fans growing in them. These cracks also have copper sweepers and bigeyes in them. Around May and June look for ornate ghost pipefish in the gorgonians. Big

Pyramid butterflyfish, Shark Pit

Agat Bay

lionfish are around the rock's front.

The entire area was a military dumpsite for years and very big sharks would congregate around the edge of the cliff looking for something to scavenge. This dumping hasn't been done in years and seeing a shark here is a rarity, but old mess hall trays and all kinds of other things once military can be found littered along the bottom.

There are two tanks at 280 feet. Up shallow, remnants of amtracs and bulldozers are found in the area.

There is a school of pyramid butterflyfish that will swarm if food is offered and bird wrasses and other familiar finned beggars will also show here for the fish photographer to capture. Look for large lionfish around to the front of the pinnacle.

When you head up to the boat, there are archeye hawkfish in the table corals up on top of the big pinnacle.

5) Eel Gardens Sand Flats

Location: Rizal Bay
Attractions: Sand Flats, Eels
Depth: 45 to 120 feet
Logistics: Boat Dive

Garden eel

Garden eels live in groups in the sand, but often divers never see them as they will retreat without a sign or sound if they hear or see divers approach. So diving the Eel Gardens requires a kind and gentle approach to diving.

Located along a huge sand wash that flows down into deep water off Rizal Bay, the site starts shallow as triggerfish swim the upper waters of this gradual dropoff. There are a couple of old cables that lead down into a large sandy plain. Once at the edge of the plain, move slowly and look for movement at the bottom of the sea floor.

Garden eels like areas with some current. They will bob back and forth from their holes catching planktonic creatures that are carried by the moving water. Approach slowly when you spot them and breath minimally as the bubbles spook them. Look closely and you will spot hundreds, maybe even thousands, feeding from the sea floor.

The area around this flat has some beautiful sea anemones and there are other fish and invertebrates, like pincushion starfish. This is a deep dive even though it may not seem like it, so keep careful to track time and depth.

6) Rizal Coral Heads

Location: Rizal Bay
Attractions: Corals, Anemones
Depth: 10 to 40 feet
Logistics: Boat Dive

At the north end of Rizal Beach are some coral heads that provide a

Juvenile boxfish

great spot for a shallow second dive or just snorkeling. On a sunny day, these shallow corals reflect the sun and provide a great backdrop for photography or just a long, exploratory dive. There are anemone schools with lots of clown damsels in them on some of the coral heads. This spot is great for the macrophotographer or videographer wanting to capture the hijinks.

The sandy patches between the heads have sea cucumbers and starfish. Also, look for the interaction between the goby and the blind shrimp that live communally, the goby acting as guardian for the ever-active hole clearing shrimp. Look also for weedlike juvenile rockmover wrasses.

This site can be reached from shore, but it is a more relaxing dive if approached by boat. Take some time to poke around in the many cracks and crannies found at the base of the coral head for invertebrates like Christmas tree worms.

7) Hap's Reef

Location: Agat Bay
Attractions: Fish and Sea Anemones
Depth: 20 to 60 feet
Logistics: Boat Dive

Hap's reef is one of Guam's unique undersea attractions. A loaf-shaped reef in the bay north of Gaan Point, it was developed by Guam tour operators and photo-minded divers. Hap's is one of the places where divers can hand feed a variety of Pacific tropical fish, and as it is in the open ocean, a good variety of fish are here.

Hap's Reef

Skunk clownfish in sea anemone

an interesting reef. So a dive on Hap's is far from disappointing.

The swirl of reef tropicals is quite breathtaking to even the most jaded diver. The reef was once home to a moray eel that was as gentle as a lap dog. Hap's has numerous sea anemones, producing an array of curious clownfish for underwater photographers.

Because of the lack of spearfishing laws in Agat Bay, it doesn't have large fish. Moorings just off the reef have been established to protect the coral.

In the early '80s, the reef was wracked by dynamite blasts and spearfishing scourges that indiscriminately killed a lot of fish and coral. Of late, these senseless acts haven't been repeated and the fish population is rebounding. The coral is not as healthy is it once was but it is still

Hap's is truly an example of many things good and bad, mostly caused by man, that can happen to a reef.

It is well worth the effort of a leisurely visit. Hap's is an especially interesting night dive with anemone hermit crabs waddling around and lots of nudibranchs in the low reef areas next to the hard coral formation. Look for moon gazers buried in the sandy pockets south of the reef.

Gaan Point

8) Gaan Point & Amtrac

Location: Agat Bay
Attractions: Coral Heads, Mini-Wall
Depth: 15 to 60
Logistics: Boat or Beach Dive

The Gaan Point site is full of large coral heads and a variety of sea anemones. Each bommie seems to have at least one anemone in or on it. The area is sometimes exposed to sewage outfall during high runoff, so it is best to dive here after it has been dry (no rain) for a couple of days. That said, beach divers can head out a sandy channel to the left of the point's pipeline that can be accessed behind the Agat Cemetery. The sand flats have a series of mini-atolls surrounded by sea grasses. There is an old Japanese boat in this channel that often attracts fish. They hover inside the upside-down hull.

The swim out has a mini-wall on the left side and channel with coral heads on the other. Occasionally, a large barracuda comes into this channel. Look for invertebrate life in the coral heads including the tiny burrowing coral hermit crabs that like this area.

Gaan Point corals

The channel opens to a broad sandy area that holds many large coral heads. The wall also continues to the left.

Each coral head has something unique to offer. Take time to look around closely. This was a major WWII invasion site as well, and even now an occasional helmet or gas mask gets uncovered in the changing sand.

Spinner dolphins surfing

The swim underwater to the amtrac at Gaan Point can be a healthy one and some people prefer to snorkel out to conserve air and see the amtrac and then make a leisurely dive back . It is not difficult to find, however, as it rests away from a point in the reef in the white sand.

The vehicle was part of the U.S. invasion force that stormed the island in 1944. It is one of many that once rested on the bottom of Agat Bay. A salvage company was contracted by the military to recover the vehicles.

Most have been removed, but this amtrac was left behind and now serves as a historical dive destination.

A little compass navigation is about all that is needed to find this war relic. The diver should go to the end of the Gaan Point pipeline and look for a large coral head in the middle of the south channel. It sits almost parallel with the end of the pipeline. Set your compass at the 270 degree heading and swim as the ‘fish swims' (crow flies) using natural navigation.

For those wanting to dive to the amtrac, part of the trip is at 20 to 30 foot depths that then gets deeper, opening to a 50 foot bottom. There is sometimes a school of sharpnose barracuda near the reef by the amtrac.

9) Coral Gardens

Location: Inner Anae Island
Attractions: Cavern, Corals, and Fish
Depth: 10 to 50 feet
Logistics: Boat Dive

Guam's varied reef structures allow divers to explore a number of different formations offshore. The most popular reefs seem to be those that are accessible, somewhat shallow and easy to reach. The Coral Gardens fit the bill.

Boat diving is recommended as it's

just a couple minutes from the Agat Marina.

The Coral Gardens are situated in the large channel that flows past Anae Island into Facpi Bay. You know you're close when you spot the rocks that break the surface near the east shore of Anae. Some corals rise very close to the surface. The beauty of diving the Gardens comes from the great variety of sites within the area.

There is no special place to anchor. Instead, the diver should make a number of trips here exploring the various formations in the channel. For instance, close to the island huge coral pillars rise as high as 25 feet from the ocean floor. An entire dive can be made exploring the various pinnacles and their accompanying sea life.

Nearer the channel, the Gardens open into a series of patch reefs with anemones and shell life.

Toward the start of the Gardens is an area of sand flats in 55 feet of water with coral and algae encrusted mounds. Starfish, moray eels and snoozing whitetip sharks are common here. Soldierfish and squirrelfish also hide under the ledges of these coral hills. And eagle rays are known to glide by.

Many dives can be made on these reefs experiencing new sea life on each dive. There are also two things to look out for at the Coral Gardens, one good... one bad.

Bad: During the trade wind months small, stinging man-o-war wash into the area. Check the water before plunging. Good: Spinner dolphins sometimes come in here and will play in the wake of the boat bow. This is an added

Anae Island

pleasure that, combined with a long dive, makes the Coral Gardens attractive. Also, if very calm, there is a cave that can be entered on Anae Island's west side and the diver can climb up and take a land tour if desired.

10) Pete's Reef

Location: Facpi Bay
Attractions: Swim-throughs, Fish and Sleeping Sharks
Depth: 20 to 80 feet
Logistics: Boat Dive

Guam's veteran undersea explorer Pete Peterson found Pete's Reef. It is a nice mix of small caves, coral heads and sandy patches that gives a good variety of marine life a home.

There are many small tunnels and nooks at Pete's that sit in 50 feet of water and can be safely passed through.

Western Sunset

Pete's Reef

anemone crabs come out. Planktonic creatures come out also and will form a cluster of frenzied action around a video light or strong dive light.

11) Agat Bay

Location: Southern Guam
Attractions: Cavern, Sea whips, Fish
Depth: 30 to 130 feet
Logistics: Boat Dives

Agat Bay is the large expanse of water running parallel to the entire village. It doesn't have an abundance of big coral heads, but rather a scattered system of patch reefs, sandy flats and channels. There are a number of popular dive sites in the bay, but much of the terrain goes unexplored.

The type of diver who might enjoy

Starfish and other invertebrates and an occasional eel likes to inhabit the inside of these mazelike holes.

There is usually a whitetip shark sleeping in the sandy bottom. The reef is open to the deep blue sea and sometimes a pelagic fish, like a dogooth tuna, will come in here.

There are many anemones in the corals and some in the sand that are worth photographing, including one unusual sand anemone at 80 feet. They host a good variety of clown damselfish.

Pete's is also a good night dive as many creatures like

Gaan Point amtrac

this area would be the amateur biologist, macrophotographer or the patient exploratory diver who takes his or her diving slowly. The barren reaches may seem uninhabited but they are actually alive with a large variety of plants and animals.

A swim to some of the 40 to 50 foot areas south of the Namo River outfall can reveal an active ocean. There is a scattering of coral heads mostly overgrown with encrusting sponges, algae, ascidians and hydroids. Tree worms dot many corals in an array of colors from sky blue to maroon and cream. They share their base with tiny coral hermit crabs whose pincers and antennae peek out of tiny holes.

Palm-size sea stars also make the flats home. They range in color from military green to peppermint striped reds and whites. Nudibranchs are found in diversity ranging in color from common blue and yellow to delicate, bulbous, veined nudis.

The sandy bottom attracts large, disclike rays with their mottled skin. I have also seen hawksbill turtles here. An occasional eagle ray also glides by to add excitement to a dive. The flats are also good for some kinds of shelling.

Dives like **Cemetery Wall** and **Scott's Point** are deep dropoffs spots for advanced divers. There is also a **WWII zero plane** at tech depths.

While Agat Bay diving isn't for everyone, it is far from boring for those who know what they want to see and look for it. And there is always the chance of being swooped by a manta ray or escorted back by dolphins.

12) Nathan's Dent

Location: South of Facpi Point
Attractions: Corals, fish life
Depth: 30 - 70 feet
Logistics: Boat Dive

MDA's Jim Miller named this site for his boatman, Nathan Dent, after an

Green moray

exploratory dive turned out to be popular. Located on the south side of Facpi Island, divers usually drop closer to the Sella Bay beach and swim with the reef on the right. Divers just drop in as this site has no mooring buoy.

A kind of S-shaped reef meanders from 35 to 70 feet with plate corals covering a steep sloping wall. Sand then runs out and down deeper.

The site has some nice swim-throughs and whitetip reef sharks, stingrays and even Napoleon wrasse like this healthy reef. There are also lots of lionfish that make the crevices and cracks home.

This is usually a good site for a dive to see marine life as it isn't visited all that much.

13) Fouha Bay

Location: North of Umatac
Attractions: Caverns, Fish
Depth: 3 to 30 feet
Logistics: Boat or Beach

Not too many folks stop at Fouha. It is not that deep and often overlooked, but there are some small caves and crevices here that are large enough to be entered and there is also some mysterious airplane wreckage that may be the remnants of a WWII plane shot down during the Great Marianas Turkey Shoot.

Located the next bay up from Umatac Bay, Fouha is at times home to spinner dolphins that stay in Guam's bays by day to rest or sleep. The bottom here is somewhat silty and covered with natural debris as it is a spillway for the Fouha River that flows down from Guam's rolling hills.

Facing the shore from the sea, the left side of the bay has some small caves that make nice sites for photography when the sun is high. Sun shafts streak through the cracks in the top of this

Fouha Bay

Spider conch eye

River empties into the sea and swim left for caves, holes and scattered coral heads.

There are numerous canyons and schools of bream and goatfish. The weaving in and out can be fun but don't penetrate too far as silt can get kicked up making

honeycombed reef and create great dances of light inside the caverns.

Schools of small sweepers make these caves home and flash in and out of sight when a light shines their way.

There is the remnant of a plane in the bay and it makes one wonder if it is part of the **Umatac Zero** or possibly part of another victim that may have crashed into the hill. The search for the rest of the plane is still on.

14) Toguan Bay

Location: Toguan River
Attractions: Caverns, Fish, Coral Heads
Depth: 10 to 60
Logistics: Beach or Boat

This is an area that is calm most of the year except when there is a southern swell. Park just off the road by the village sign at the bridge, dress and wade across the reef flat. Enter the water at the shelf where the small Toguan

for an uncomfortable exit if you meet a dead end.

There is a mini-wall of healthy coral and a big coral head with a large anemone and other invertebrate life farther south. Explore the sandy outer reaches and look for mottled rays, shells and an occasional shark. Spinner dolphins also come into this area and at special times their calls can be heard. They rarely approach divers. They seem to dislike the bubbles.

This can be a good night dive with cowries and other shell life coming out of the caves to feed.

Toguan Bay

15) Cocos Island Lagoon

Location: Southern barrier reef
Attractions: Invertebrates, corals, fish
Depth: 2 to 30 feet
Logistics: Beach or boat dive

The sandy flats and scattered coral heads inside the Cocos barrier reef in southern Guam offer fascinating snorkeling or diving for the patient and curious. While not blessed with the more ornate formations found in Agat's Coral Gardens, this area is very much alive with marine life, especially from the smaller end of the animal world. The sea grasses that grow inside the lagoon offer protection for a number of juvenile animals not ready to venture into the competitive world of the coral reef. Everything from miniature octopus to young barracuda and skipjack can be seen in this environment.

Critters are apt to remain undercover in this environment. Small anemones can be seen waving from holes in scattered rocks and coral heads. Banded shrimp have set up cleaning stations and the sharp-eyed observer can also spot the translucent glass shrimp. There are bristleworms in many sizes and pastel colors, file shells (disco clams) with their flowing tentacles and clinging shells either full or with a hermit crab. Look for frogfish and leaf fish in the staghorn coral beds.

The Bikini island area, the small sand spit next to Cocos, has stands of staghorn coral that protect blue chromis and anemone colonies There are also a lot of burrowing crabs in the area.

There is a Manila Galleon sunk off Cocos Island with millions of dollars of gold and silver specie aboard. Despite intense exploration, the motherload remains undiscovered.

16) Cocos Wall

Location: Outside Cocos Island
Attractions: Wall, Sea whips, Fish
Depth: 40 to 130 feet
Logistics: Boat Dive

Cocos Island sits at Guam's southernmost tip and is swept by almost constant currents as the Pacific Ocean and the Philippine Sea meet and sweep south to other reefs and sea mounts south of the island.

There is a wall, or actually a strongly pitched slope, along the outer edge of Cocos Island that provides a glimpse at some beautiful sea life and an occasional pelagic fish. The more fantastic sea life is at the deep end of the diving scale here.

There are golden sea fans along the wall. The wall can have a varied current depending on the moon and the time of day. These gorgonians are a deep yellow (below) when illuminated by a strong light or the strobe of an underwater camera. Looking up through the clear water at the whips and the sun reminds a diver of the dropoffs of Palau. Look for jacks and schools of sharpnose barracuda that may come in out of curiosity to see who is diving the wall.

Cocos Wall sea fans

Piti Bay

Guam's Marine Preserves

Juvenile eagle ray

Guam's preserves are new to the island. In recent years, the betterment of Guam's diverse underwater world has been the thrust behind a series of nature preserves set up around the island. Far-sighted people in neighboring Palau set aside its 70 Islands Nature Preserve in the late 1950s. Guam's little series of marine oasis are around ten years old, with strict enforcement and staffing coming only in the last few years. They are already deemed a success, with fish populations noticeably increasing within these special reefs areas.

In the past, overfishing, siltation from poorly planned development and typhoons have all played a part in threatening Guam's marine life. There has been a sharp decline in large, mature breeding fish over last 20 years on the island. So reducing threats to Guam's somewhat fragile marine resources has become a major goal for the biologists at the island's Division of Aquatic and Wildlife Management.

Fishing is kept to a minimum in these areas, allowing breeding stocks to prosper to produce more fish.

Achang & Sasa Preserves

The preserves include the **Achang Reef Flat** in southern Guam, southeast of Cocos Island. This area is a prime spot for young fish to grow, as there are many mangroves and other natural

Camel Rock

protections for the juveniles. Moving up the western coast, the **Sasa Bay** is another mangrove area in the eastern part of Apra Harbor.

This has long been a breeding ground for fish including hammerhead sharks. These two areas are not recreational spots, but are important to providing a place for mature fish to spawn and for young fish to grow in safety. The fish that move out to sea from here not only populate Guam, but some migrate to outer islands, like the atolls of Yap State.

Piti Bay Preserve

The two most popular and well-used spots are The Piti Bomb Holes, which actually includes most of Piti Bay including Camel Rock, Fish Eye Marine Park and the Piti Channel, and Tumon Bay. Piti Bay is another prime site for fish with over 200 species in this compact area inside the reef.

This is one of Guam's most accessible sites, a favorite of introductory scuba divers and snorkelers. It has sandy sink holes, glorious soft and hard coral growth, much of which is decades old,

and lots of fish. The fish include seven different butterflyfish species, eagle rays and the occasional sea turtle. Nurse and Whitetip sharks can be found over the reef in the outer reef fingers.

Divers and underwater photographers are amazed at how approachable the fish are here. This is one of Guam's most accessible sites and is a favorite of introductory scuba divers and snorkelers. Snorkeling and SeaWalker tours take place daily and the Fish Eye Undersea Observatory brings the sea to those who want to see the ocean from the facility's windows.

Divers can see the healthy reef on the south side of the observatory, feed the fish and even snorkel around the observatory itself. Fish Eye has a snorkel tour that has seven stops and looks at various fish life, different kinds of corals and also a sea anemone colony with clownfish. There is a resident pufferfish just under the entry and exit platform at Fish Eye. Afterwards, take a trip inside the observatory or visit the gift shop in the Fish Eye facility across the street.

Double saddle butterflyfish

Tumon Bay Preserve

Perhaps best known is Tumon Bay, including the areas around Gun Beach and Two Lover's Point. The preserve sits on Guam's premiere beach, lined by hotels, clubs and dining venues. It's blue waters offer all kinds of recreation from competitive paddling and swimming to local cast (talaya) net fishing and snorkeling. The inner reef at Tumon is like a miniature aquarium, with many colorful tropical reefs.

Fiddler crab

Ocean currents, making the sea full of nutrients and thus, a good site for young fish to prosper, constantly flush these protected waters.

North of here and still within the preserve, **Gun Beach**, is considered a fun boat dive or beach dive. Named for the WWII gun

Pati Point Preserve

emplacement near the cliffline that sits on its shore, this sloping reef has a lot of fish life and is great for fish photography. Sea turtles, marble rays, manta rays and even the rare tiger shark have been seen off the shores.

The site's buoy is near a healthy coral garden of castle corals. The reef slopes down and bottoms out at about 110 feet to a sandy plain. Look for possible garden eels and helmet shells in the depths.

Healthy coral gardens are found to the left. Manta rays have been known to come here to feed on the outgoing tide at the major cut in the Tumon Bay reef.

Pati Point Preserve

The final area is known as Pati Point in northern Guam. This site was set aside a while ago by the military and the results are refreshing. There are schooling fish, sea turtles and lots of other signs that preserves do work at the Pati site. The corals here are also quite healthy and the view of Guam's coastline makes this a fine place to visit. Waves and strong currents discourage beach diving and make it hard to come here by boat on a consistent basis, which is probably good for the fish.

The preserves are trying to reduce fishing pressure. For over a decade, biologists studied Guam's reefs and decided that the increased population on the island meant more fishermen.

The preserves have been called egg banks, places where fish can lay and hatch youngsters without predation from man.

A superb investment in Guam's future, the preserves could use more support and even more preserve areas.

Piti Bomb Holes

17) Piti Channel

Location: West of USO, Piti Village
Attractions: Corals, fish feeding
Depth: 30 feet
Logistics: Shore dive

Piti Channel is sometimes the first dive made for those learning to dive on Guam. It is used by instructors because it isn't too deep but still offers a good experience and its sandy bottom allows divers to practice new skills. But it should not be dismissed as just a beginner's place. For safety, stay away from the seaward underpass on the power plant side. Divers have drowned here.

This channel has a lot of invertebrate creatures for the macrophotographer to shoot like glass shrimp, harlequin shrimp, hermit crabs, tree worms and rarely a seahorse. Stonefish of various sizes, shapes and colors stay here too.

This is also a good night dive place as Spanish dancers and various brilliantly colored flatworms come out of hiding.

In the bay, the channel entrance is a favorite gathering site for eagle rays at outgoing tide. I would recommend diving the channel mouth by boat, however, as the currents closer to the channel mouth can become quite strong and sweep a diver out to sea. The inner channel is rarely a problem.

18) Piti Bomb Holes Preserve

Location: Piti shoreline, Guam
Attractions: Corals, fish feeding
Depth: 35 feet
Logistics: Shore dive

Piti's Bomb Holes are easily recognizable as one drives south on Marine Drive and enters the village of Piti. Located inside the reef, the holes take on a deep blue caste surrounded by varying shades of turquoise. They are as appealing to snorkel or dive in as they are to view from the land. They are not deep and the highly reflective white sand bottom makes for a colorful dive.

Butterflyfish

In reality, the Bomb Holes probably were not caused by the war. Richard Randall, formerly of the UOG Marine Lab, says they are most likely collapsed caves that are part of Guam's honeycombed crust. They have filled with sand and sea and offer an easy and accessible dive.

Juvenile parrotfish

To reach the holes, one can wade along the Fish Eye Marine Park observatory pier or snorkel, depending on the tide, to the edge. The northernmost hole is the largest and most popular with divers. The reef flat near the hole has a number of soft corals growing on it. There is also a type of sand sea anemone here that resembles soft coral and retracts quickly when touched. This is toxic to humans and touching it should be avoided.

The sand flats also produce another stinging creature, the cone shell. This animal is has a poison barb it can actually fire like arrow. Do not handle the shells.

One other thing to watch out for, at some high tides a rip current can run.

Piti Bay corals

through the flats and make the going tough. Care should be taken when swimming out to negotiate the flow without tiring yourself out before you get to the dive.

The sandy slope leading into the hole is pure white and holds many small sand dwellers. The hole is a maximum of about 35 feet deep and contains a number of large coral heads. In the nooks and crooks of the corals there are moray eels and octopi.

Moorish idols and small butterflyfish are seen abundantly during the day. Pipefish skirt the top of the coral heads and needlefish skim the water overhead, swimming just below the surface and following the diver's bubbles.

Fish feeding takes places here and there are big jacks, snapper schools and plenty of butterflyfish that inhabit different levels of the cascading reef.

The Bomb Holes can also be a nice spot for night diving. During a full moon, the white sand acts as a reflector so you can turn off your light and experience the surreal ambiance.

Goatfish at cleaning station

In all, the Bomb Holes are a good area for snorkelers and beginning divers to sharpen their skills. Even the 'old pros' enjoy this site for a hassle-free, relaxing way to view the undersea world.

19) Asan Cut and War in the Pacific National Historical Park
Location: Asan Village shoreline
Attractions: Corals, caves, and flats
Depth: 20 to 120 feet
Logistics: Shore dive

Asan Cut is located adjacent to War in the Pacific NHP in Asan. It is a dive that can only be done under ideal conditions. The reef configuration makes this place dangerous during times of even moderate surf. Currents and siltation that causes poor visibility are both easily formed here.

July is one of the better times of the year to venture in here. Parking in the small local park puts you in close proximity with the shore. There are a few trees and picnic areas for shade. Nearby the War in the Pacific National Historical Park is too much of a walk from the parking area for a beach dive.

The entry point is pretty obvious as the reef forms a 'V' along the top of the reef flat. Go out to the big rock and head in. The reef drops to about 20 feet, making it easy to slide into the water. The Asan River empties onto the reef close by. The best visibility is to the south, but there is an amtrac (amphibious tractor) remaining from the Second World War to the north in about 25 feet of water. If you want to see it, it may be best to snorkel to it, make a short dive and then head for clearer and deeper water to the south.

Asan was an invasion site for American troops and many people lost their lives during this fierce battle. Even today the surf kicks up war remnants and divers will spot spent and live

Hospital Point

ammunition on the sand bottom and along the reef. Sea turtles are also reported here. The more scenic diving here is the swim to the left. This area is similar to Toguan Bay. There aren't as many caves, but the bottom levels out to sand at 60-120 feet and interspersed along the bottom are immense coral heads, some rising to a Medusalike 50 feet to within 10 feet of the surface.

Near the shoreline there are schools of herbivorous fishes. On one dive I also saw a school of large squid along the surfline. The bottom is noted for having small tunicates, hydroids and other such attached invertebrates.

20) Hospital Point

Location: Tamuning cliffline
Attractions: Corals, sea fans, and pelagics
Depth: 20 to 130 feet
Logistics: Boat dive

Hospital Point's untouched sea fans remind the diver of dropoffs in Palau. It is a deep but beautiful dive conveniently located in central Guam off the Tamuning/Tumon cliffline. Obviously, it is a dive in the area below

Double saddle butterflyfish

Convict tangs

the point where the hospital (GMH) is built. The major attractions are the clear, blue water, a sloping dropoff punctuated with caves, sea fans and sea whips, and the possibility of sighting large pelagic fish like tuna, barracuda, bumphead parrotfish and sharks. This area is dived so little and is so immediately adjacent to the open sea that I wouldn't be surprised to hear about sightings of dolphins, sailfish, marlins or other large sea critters not usually seen along other parts of Guam's barrier reefs. A humpback whale and calf was sighted along here once and the pair stayed close to shore for two days.

The dive is most conveniently done from the Agana Boat Basin. The cliffs drop sharply into the sea. They provide habitat for sea birds and coconut crabs. The dropoff isn't severe but it is pronounced. The best way to dive this site is by boatman. Currents here can be strong and tricky at times, non-existent at others. Having someone up top is the smartest way to dive here as the few shore entries are long swims from shore. Swim along the gradual dropoff starting at the deepest part of your dive and gradually move up.

When entering the water, drop down and slowly reach the depth you desire. The water here is extremely clear and it is easy to go beyond your planned depth, so keep an eye on your gauges

and computer.

The sand bottom along the drop is probably 250 feet deep or more. It quickly falls to 600 then 1200 feet. Diving at about 100 feet will allow the diver to see sea fans and a variety of reef fish. Clown triggerfish like this steep slope as do schools of pyramid butterflyfish that like to congregate along the edges of deepwater dropoffs.

Sea anemones are found at shallower depths, like 60 feet. They sometimes play host to Clark's anemonefish, the white tailed clownfish rarely seen except along the deeper dropoffs.

Swimming up at the end of the dive for a safety decompression, the many cracks and crevices near the cliffline are the home for scores of tiny baitfish that attract skipjacks. The jacks will dart in and out of the silvery fish in water just five to ten feet deep. Moray eels live in the holes in the pocked corals and other anemones also make their homes here.

Beware of the surge if the seas or swells are up.

The boatman can easily follow your bubbles in the clear water and you merely need to surface and hop on board for a trip back to mainland Guam.

21) Tumon Bay
Location: Tumon Bay
Attractions: Bright tropicals, coral thickets
Depth: 5 to 15 feet
Logistics: Beach dive
Level: Snorkel, novice, advanced, macro or fish photographer

Tumon Bay is the ideal place for the fishwatcher to ply his or her trade. Tumon is an outdoor aquarium of sorts with many of the area's most common marine tropicals in abundance. Some not-so-common fish also will appear to those who put in the diving or

Tumon Bay & Hilton

Tumon Bay

snorkeling time. Tumon Bay is the area that runs from the Nikko Hotel to the Hilton International Guam. Part of the marine preserve, it has shallow reef flats, patch coral, coral thickets and bright, white sand flats. Probably the most popular dive or snorkeling site is at the bay's southern end at Ypao Beach. This is one of the deeper areas within Tumon as it was purposely dredged for swimming. A lifeguard is on duty here and most of the time hazards like windsurfers and jet skiers are shooed away from the location. This hole is filled with branching corals of the staghorn variety. They provide habitat, food, breeding and spawning areas. The growth becomes thicker as one swims toward the outer reef and brilliant blue damsels known as chromis become abundant. They feed in an active school just below the surface and their shiny silver sides reflect the sun's rays. When a snorkeler approaches too closely, they will form a tighter formation and dive for the safety of the staghorn thicket.

Longnose filefish

Other species including juvenile squirrelfish, tangs,

butterflyfish, long-nosed filefish and the eel-like pipefish also use the staghorn branches for protection. The pipefish, by the way, is a close cousin of the seahorse. The male actually incubates the eggs in a ventral pouch until they hatch, just as seahorses do. Pipefishes are quite common on Tumon.

Other areas of Tumon also have much to offer. There is a diverse eel population in the sandy reef flats. The honeycomb provides prime habitat for many species like the snowflake eel, spotted morays and the foul-tempered viper moray. Is there anything bigger here? Stingrays have been seen here and also flying gurnards. At the cut near Outrigger, manta rays are regularly reported but jet skiing can make this an unsafe place to dive. In all, Tumon is a fine place for aspiring fish photographers who want to spend a long time underwater and for those who just like to look around at the sea.

22) Gun Beach

Location: Gun Beach Cut
Attractions: Invertebrates, coral heads
Depth: 20 to 120 feet
Logistics: Beach or Boat

Gun Beach is one of Guam's most accessible dives and a popular site for watching a great variety of fish and other large creatures when conditions are right and people help the process. Manta rays and even dolphins are seen here on occasion.

Manta reflections

Double Reef

Located in front of the Nikko Hotel next to Fai Fai Beach, the Gun Beach is named for the WWII Japanese shore gun found along the cliffline. Tumon was never invaded, so in all likelihood, it was never fired in battle. The area was shelled by Americans, however. There appear to be parts of an airplane high up on the cliff. Local historians believe it is what is left of as victim of the Great Marianas Turkey Shoot, an immense U.S. victory held over Guam.

Most people enter through the cable cut at Gun Beach. When surf is low, this is the easiest way. A nasty rip forms here when water is high, however, making returning difficult, so keep this in mind.

There are nice coral formations in 25 to 50 feet of water to the south. There are large holes to the north. There are sea anemones in the area and crevalle jacks often come in to feed. Some fish feeding is done here, so fish photos are possible. They do feed fish near the mooring buoy to the left of the cut and so some fish are friendly. There are sharks and large barracuda seen here occasionally.

23) Double Reef

Location: Northwest Coast
Attractions: Corals, Sand Flats, and Fish
Depth: 5 to 70 feet
Logistics: Boat Dive

The ride to Double Reef is sometimes as much fun as the diving when one gets there. The normal plan of action is to make a day of it as the setting is tranquil and the underwater terrain is quite scenic. On the way up, go near the Tanguisson outfall as mantas like to

Pati Point Preserve

feed here on the surface in the mornings. You can snorkel and watch.

The Double Reef area lies just offshore near Pugua Point. An old military dumpsite is probably what caused the large, green cliff to be treeless in front of the reef. It makes a good landmark. The break on the second reef is usually quite apparent. The fringing inner reef is near a small, sandy beach that is carved out of the cliffline. There is a cave here that can be snorkeled.

Most Double Reef dives are at a safe sport diving depth, allowing for plenty of bottom time. An offshore current occasionally picks up along the deeper, less protected reefs and should be respected. Because much of the terrain has heavy coral growth, it tends to start looking the same and a compass is a good companion in getting around on long, explorative dives.

The reefs have a lot of variety, interspersed with fingerlike sand flats. When seen from the air, the deep blue of the outer dropoff quickly blends into the various shades of turquoise for an extremely colorful picture. I have seen from a helicopter a large pod of spinner dolphins playing in the morning in this shallow oasis.

Double Reef has large sand pits in about 30 feet of water. The surrounding coral is thick and many spots sport growth so competitive that different species have grown into one another

24) Pati Point

Location: Offshore North Coast
Attractions: Pelagics, Tunnel, Schools
Depth: 30 to 100 feet
Logistics: Boat Dive

The final marine preserve area is known as Pati Point in northern Guam on the Air Force base. This site was set aside a while ago by the military and the results are refreshing.

There are schooling fish, sea turtles and lots of other signs that preserves do work at the Pati site. The corals here are also quite healthy and the view of Guam's coastline makes this a fine place to visit.

The highlight is a big, sea fan filled tunnel that can have a healthy current running through it. Look for sleeping whitetips. Waves and strong currents make it hard to come here on a consistent basis and beach diving is asking for trouble. Dive here by boat.

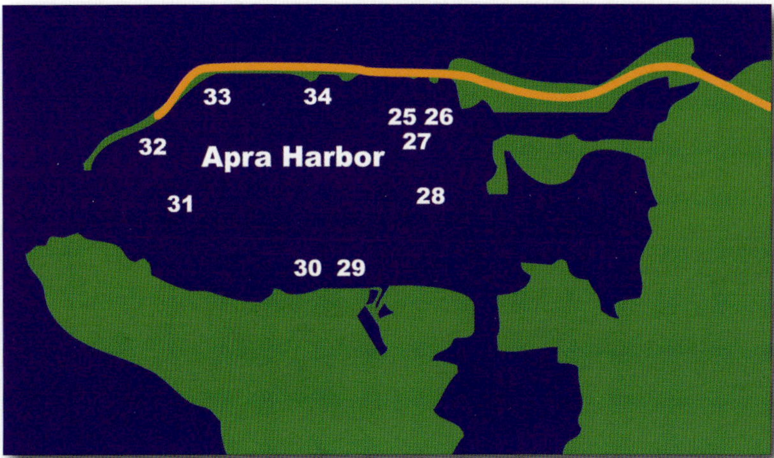

Apra Harbor

25) Tokai Maru
26) SMS Cormoran
27) Kitsugawa Maru
28) Western Shoals
29) GabGab Beach
30) GabGab II Reef
31) Hidden Reef
32) Seabee Junkyard
33) American Tanker
34) Family Beach

Apra Harbor

The WRECKS

Guam has a number of diveable shipwrecks and airplanes that were sunk during the battles of World War II. Guam was a major invasion site for American forces retaking the island. It was the first U.S. possession taken captive during that conflict as it was invaded as Pearl Harbor in Hawaii was being bombed. The retaking of Guam came three years later as the island was shelled heavily for weeks, air battles grounded Japanese planes and then invasion troops stormed much of the southern and central western coasts. Remnants of those battles, from bullets to bombs, are still found today in the hills and by unsuspecting, and often alarmed, bulldozer operators.

Tokai Maru

Tokai Maru wash basin area

25) Tokai Maru

Location: Apra Harbor
Attractions: Sunken WWII ship, Fish
Depth: 40 to 125 feet
Logistics: Boat dive

Just east of the green marker buoy nearest the old seaplane ramp on the Breakwater side of the harbor sits the Tokai Maru. It is a Japanese freighter sunk by a submarine torpedo attack during World War II. Oddly enough, it rests on a ship, the Cormoran, which was scuttled during World War I. Thus, two victims of two different world wars rest touching in the harbor. Nowhere else in the world can this combination be found, allowing the diver to visit ships from two different wars in one dive.

The Tokai is by far the more popular of the two as it is shallow enough to overswim in one dive. This ship sits at a list and can be somewhat disorienting. The bridge area is quite open and the combination of the maze of crossmembers and the slant of the ship have confused many a diver. There is not much to see inside except an old wash area with a tiled floor and sink. The shafts of light coming through the doorways and beams make a nice scene, however.

The Tokai is not overgrown with coral, although it does have nice growth in some spots. The bow area has black and orange rope sponges growing along the rail and drain areas. For many divers, this is a blessing because the ship is still recognizable and it is easy to get an idea what the ship looked like.

The Tokai was a big freighter. It is about 500 feet long. The bow holds the scars of an explosion and jagged metal must be watched for. Her anchor chain is out and there are many cables and some winches on deck.

As it is a natural reef and also very close to another shallow harbor reef, there are a lot of fish around the wreck. A good way to observe fish here is to go out on the end of the smoke stacks and watch them school. At the right time of day there can be a good deal of action taking place in the open water.

26) SMS Cormoran

Location: Apra Harbor
Attractions: Sunken WWI ship, Fish
Depth: 70 to 125 feet
Logistics: Boat dive

Apra Harbor today

The SMS Cormoran started claiming lives the day it sank. Seven crewmen died after its captain agreed to peacefully surrender the crew but not give up the ship.

On the first day of World War I, April l7, 1917, a U.S. Navy lieutenant was ordered to demand the ship's surrender. The German Cormoran had been in internment in Apra Harbor for a couple of years. The ship's crew had become friendly with their American military counterparts. So the lieutenant left the Cormoran reluctantly when he heard the captain was unwilling to surrender the ship. He didn't have to wait long to find out what the next move would be. As he was leaving in a skiff, the Cormoran's captain gave orders to abandon ship.

An explosion was then heard and smoke, flames and flying debris was seen behind the bridge. The ship reportedly went down quickly, in less than 5 minutes after the initial explosion. Crew members were abandoning ship from the stern. It listed heavily to starboard, sitting horizontally, and then sunk.

Seven crew members drowned before they could be picked up by a U.S. rescue ship. One was never found. The other six were buried in a little used Naval cemetery that now sits in East Agana along the ocean side of Marine Drive.

In 1975, local author and diver Herb Ward, who wrote a book about the ship called 'The Flight of the Cormoran', also died while exploring the Cormoran. In 1980 another diver was diving inside the ship when he lost his life after the compartment he was exploring silted over and he ran out of air trying to find his way out.

This ship was actually the 'new' Cormoran, a Russian mail ship captured in August of 1914 off the coast of China. She was built in China in 1909. After capture she was quickly converted to replace the 'old' Cormoran, an outmoded gunboat known well in China and Micronesia. She plied the seas for Germany in this part of the world and was capable of carrying a crew of 350. But she was surrounded by enemies and supplies and fuel became difficult to obtain. The captain accepted internment in Guam, which was a neutral base at the time.

Kitsugawa Maru bow

This ship is easily found as the Tokai Maru sits right on top of it. Just swim down past the Tokai bridge along the starboard side down. Swim all the way down the east side of the Tokai from about midships to the bow. The Cormoran will be down there.

There isn't a lot to see as the holds are empty. Some fish make this ship their home and schooling jacks and fusiliers are often seen in the area. There is a lion claw bathtub and the wooden planking still remains on some floor areas. Most of the portholes have been removed. The bowgun was taken years ago and is believed to be on display at a U.S. military installation. This ship is now protected by law and removal of artifacts is against the law. Instructors have strung ropes in these ships and use them for wreck diving training.

The Cormoran is a great part of Guam and world history. Just remember that it is deep, it is a shipwreck and it is silty and should be treated with a vast amount of respect

27) Kitsugawa

Location: Apra Harbor
Attractions: Japanese shipwreck
Depth: 60 to 130
Logistics: Boat dive

Deep in the waters of Apra Harbor sits a mysterious and fascinating shipwreck. Once you're on the Kitsugawa, you take the channel visibility gamble. On those rare days of great vis, what's left of the entire ship can come into view at about 50 feet. On the more usual days, visibility will be closer to 50 feet and may even be 30. This is still no problem as the ship is interesting to overswim.

I don't suggest penetration unless a well-thought plan has been devised. This ship is deep and the tables must be wholly respected here.

Its stern is mangled. Air strike records indicate six definite hits midships. The report says pilots did not see any apparent damage, but on a later strike, she was reported sunk. One guess is that damage was extensive enough to make her list and the cool sea water hit the hot boilers. The resulting explosion destroyed the stern. Or, the stern may have been hit in the strike.

The front mast and a cargo boom are still intact on the Kitsugawa . These are covered with salmon-colored tubastrea corals. Some of the lines leading to the upper structures are still intact also.

Most divers like to visit the bowgun, which has managed to elude salvors all of these years. The ammunition in the boxes in back of the gun is live and is very, very unstable. It should be left alone. An octopus sometimes lives in one of the empty ammo holes. At the right time of day the gun can be a fine photographic prop. A shot of the mast and perhaps a diver in the background with the gun in the fore is an enticing image. The bowgun is around 110 feet.

Railings and other ship machinery can also be seen on an overswim. Once again, take care to keep track of bottom time on this ship.

28) Western Shoals
Location: East harbor shoals
Attractions: Sponges, coral, fish
Depth: 10 to 80 feet
Logistics: Boat dive

Located in Guam's Apra Harbor, Western Shoals provides divers with opportunity to experience Guam's coral world in an environment accessible to divers most of the year. Marked by a large cement block on its northern end, this reef is a honeycombed combination of branching and plating corals, a variety of sponges, and provides shelter for Pacific reef fish common to Guam. What is different about Western Shoals is the fact that it's sponges are *(continued on Page 72)*

Castle corals

Photos pages 68 thru 71 - US National Archives
Some historical information courtesy War In The Pacific National Historical Park website

Guam's Ocean & War History

The War Comes to Guam

Only hours after Pearl Harbor was attacked, the Japanese began aerial bombings on Guam. After two days of strafing, the Japanese came ashore and hours later the naval governor surrendered the American territory. The island remained under Japanese control for 31 months until July 21, 1944 when the United States returned and liberated the island. Many lives were lost and the suffering was great for all those involved in the battles on Guam and throughout the Pacific theater. In order to remember the United State's and Guam's involvement in World War II, War in the Pacific National Historical Park, a multi-unit park located mainly in Asan, Piti and Agat villages, was established in 1978 to commemorate the bravery and sacrifice of those participating in the campaigns of the Pacific Theater of World War II.

The Maritime History

Guam waters have seen visitors since before the time of Christ. The Chamorro indigenous population are believed to have come to the island from Malaysia about 4,000 years ago. Much is still being discovered about these robust early settlers but it is believed they established trading routes

Tanks on Agat Beach

with other islanders around Micronesia and possibly around the Pacific. They were great sailors who used fast canoes to fish the inner bays and dropoffs of Guam.

Archeologists have found numerous fishing hooks reflecting different and sophisticated styles of fishing in the latte stone areas where Chamorro made their settlements. Most villages were coastal and remnants show they used the sea for both food and presumably recreation.

Ferdinand Magellan made the first European contact with Guam in 1521. It was a rude introduction that left some Umatac residents dead or with homes ablaze. Magellan's rudeness was quickly answered on his next stop when was killed in the Philippines

But news of Guam was brought back with the ship and Spain began colonizing the island in 1668. It served as an important stop for provisions and rest on the Manilla galleon trade route between Mexico and the Philippines. Manila Galleons were much larger than the Spanish galleons that plied the Atlantic and Caribbean. They carried a lot of raw products that were sent through Asia to be fashioned into high quality carvings and jewelry. Guam has the remnants of at least three of these Manila ships below its waters as does Rota and Saipan, with at least one each. The Guam wreck near Cocos Island is believed to be one of the richest wrecks in the world with a cargo of gold and silver. The motherload has yet to be found.

In 1898, the United States took control of the island following the Battle

US troops come ashore in Agat

of Guam in the Spanish-American War.

During World War II, the Japanese invaded Guam and treated the people of Guam as enemies in an occupied territory. The United States retook the island in 1944. Along the beaches in Piti, Asan and Agat, fighting was fierce. Once taken, Guam became a major hub for both air and sea endeavors as the United States worked its way toward Japan.

Eventually, atomic bombs were flown from Tinian and dropped on Hiroshima and Nagasaki, but not before more battles secured Saipan and Iwo Jima.

Guam's waters are filled with reminders of past military conflicts and naval battles involving the WWI Germans and WWII Japanese. There are wrecks of ships, planes, barges and their cargos and contents including munitions.

One of the most popular dive spots on Guam is in Apra Harbor where shipwrecks from two world wars lie adjacent to each other. The SS Rjasan was a steel hulled passenger and freight steamer built in 1909 for the Russians. The Germans captured the vessel in

Tokai Maru bow

1914, renamed it SMS Cormoran, and converted it to an armed commerce raider. From 1914 to 1917, the Cormoran sat in Apra Harbor for lack of fuel. The ship was scuttled by its captain in 1917 to avoid capture by the Americans during World War I.

The Tokai Maru was a Japanese passenger and freight steamer built in 1930. In 1941, the Japanese Imperial

Aratama Maru in Talofofo Bay

Apra Harbor & Piti

Navy re-commissioned it under contract to transport personnel and war materials. The Tokai Maru was anchored in Apra Harbor when, in January 1943, it was torpedoed and disabled by the U.S. submarine Flying Fish. Seven months later, a second U.S. submarine, the Snapper, torpedoed it again, this time sinking it. The wreck of the Tokai Maru lies adjacent to and touching in one place the wreck of the SMS Cormoran in Apra Harbor.

Other World War II underwater sites in Apra Harbor include the Japanese transports Kitsugawa Maru and Nichiyu Maru, a Japanese carrier dive bomber, and an American concrete barge sunk during the war to act as a breakwater.

The Japanese transport Aratama Maru was sunk in 1944 in Talofofo Bay on the southeastern shore of Guam (see post war photo on Page 70).

Today, the primary responsibility for underwater sites falls to the Guam Historic Preservation Office in the Department of Parks and Recreation, which partners with many federal and local entities to protect and preserve.

Agat invasion beach

Giant trevally - GabGab II

quite large in comparison to those found on the outer reefs. An occasional turtle has been seen streaking a diver here and fish feeding has been initiated by local divemasters. This last fact offers scuba buffs a chance to get closer to the reef's inhabitants and gives underwater photographers subjects that aren't as timid as those on heavily spearfished reefs.

A typical dive starts shallow. Staghorn coral covers many areas of the reeftop and schools of blue chromis make the water shimmer in brilliant shades of pastel blue.

Descending, many cuts and crevices in layered coral appear. Hidden in the recesses are Moorish idols, vertical trumpetfish (some brilliant yellow) and curious soldierfish. The underside of the coral is festooned with encrusting sponges in yellow, purple and orange.

40 feet is a good depth to observe life on Western Shoals. There are sea anemones with skunk clownfish and large carpet anemones with two-stripe clowns as residents. In one area there are a number of bulbous anemones that host no fish but resemble one of those slow-motion shots of a drop of milk landing in a glass. Western Shoals has much to offer.

29) GabGab Beach
Location: Southern Apra Shore
Attractions: Cascading Reef, Fishes, and Marine Life
Depth: 10 to 80 feet
Logistics: Beach Dive

The southern side of the Apra Harbor is a natural cascading wall of hard corals and crevices that is part of Guam's main Naval Station. This entire shoreline has some nice diving but the area south of the swimming area, called GabGab Beach, has some particularly nice areas where plenty of exploration can be done.

Explore the sloping walls along the northern slopes of the Orote Peninsula. Covered in all types of porites corals, these reefs have deep canyons and cascading coral formations that make every turn a new adventure.

Look for unicornfish and squid as well as a number of sea anemones. Tusked wrasse fish are seen here as are Moorish idols and plenty of sergeant major fish.

30) GabGab II

Location: Off Apra South Shore
Attractions: Corals, Submarine, Fish
Depth: 30 to 90 feet
Logistics: Beach or Boat Dive

This reef is the main dive site of the Atlantis Submarine and fish feeders work here daily to entertain sub guests. So this reef has lots of fish life. Just out from GabGab Beach, this coral encrusted pinnacle has some excellent sponge formations.

The lower areas of the reef have big blue elephant ear sponges that host small goby fish. There are also dripping vase sponges and round barrel sponges that come in shades of chocolate brown. Another type of sponge here is bright red but looks brown underwater until illuminated by a light of photo flash.

Divers generally come to reeftop to watch the fish feeding show when the submarine pulls into the fish station. There's a spectacular resident school of batfish. Big giant trevally come in to scavenge and nurse sharks show up to steal a meal too. A huge eel and a large hawksbill turtle live on the reef. Plus, sponges galore and some cool reef coral attracting balls.

31) Hidden Reef

Location: Near Harbor Mouth
Attractions: Corals, Anemones, Fish
Depth: 40 to 100 feet
Logistics: Boat Dive

A healthy reef in the mouth of the Apra Harbor has shelves of hard corals and good fish life. This site isn't visited that often by divers and surprises can happen here. Great hammerhead sharks are even seen here on occasion. Look for pyramid butterflyfish and numerous sea anemones on the reef.

Sea turtle & corals

The reef has cascading corals that are quite healthy and home to squirrelfish and bigeye soldierfish. The calcareous algae that grows here is also a great place to find nudibranchs and smaller invertebrates that feed or hide in this cover. Small stonefish and even pipefish like this habitat.

There are some military remnants on the reef as well that have nice sponge life growing on them.

32) SeaBee Junkyard

Location: Apra Harbor
Attractions: Old war and other relics
Depth: 40 to 130
Logistics: Boat dive

Located almost at the end of the Glass Breakwater, there is a lone tree that points out the best place to anchor to visit the dumping grounds of bulldozers, amtracs, pipes and a lot other paraphernalia that has been

American tanker

dubbed the SeaBee Junkyard. Aside from all of the vehicular debris, there also appears to be remnants of the Caribia scattered about. This was a large ocean liner that drifted during a storm into the mouth of Apra Harbor as it was being towed to Taiwan for salvage. It was subsequently salvaged there.

This is a good dive for all levels of diver as it is shallow (averages 25 to 35 feet), there is rarely a strong current of any sort, it has some interesting sites and there are some historical aspects to the site with the old landing craft that are scattered around.

It can be reached by boat by going west of the American Tanker buoy and anchoring in the shallow water below the tree. The land slopes sharply down and then flattens out at about 25 feet. There are small coral heads in the area and one amtrac is partially buried. Presumably it was already sunken when the Breakwater was built and was covered with some of the fill material.

Set some compass headings and do some natural navigation. Four bulldozers are in close proximity to one another and one large amtrac is still in good shape with room for a diver to sit in the driver's seat. Truck beds and wheels are present. There are lots of other things here, too, that were dumped as scrap that are now artificial reefs for fish and invertebrates.

The reef drops sharply and some nice plating coral growth can be seen in places along the dropoff. Turtles and an occasional shark have also been reported in deeper water past the Junkyard.

33) American Tanker

Location: Glass Breakwater
Attractions: WWII Remnant Ship
Depth: 35 to 95 feet
Logistics: Beach or Boat Dive

A very fishy wreck, this big water tanker is a remnant of WWII. This tanker was probably sunk here on purpose after the war as part of the building of the Glass Breakwater. The entire northern peninsula in the harbor was built after the war and there are other small wrecks, barges and other remnants all along this break.

Descending the buoy line to the ship, an open "bridge" area and massive rudder make the aft fun to explore. Dive guides sometimes feed fish here and there are lots of fish to greet divers as a result.

This ship should not be entered as the inside is massive and pitch black and not for sport diving. But the various

Elephant ear sponge

structures on the deck hold fish life and the bow has various coral. On the blue tunicates, look really close and you may see some tiny, transparent skeleton shrimp. Macrophotographers love to see this kind of rare invertebrate.

The reef next to the tanker is great to explore. There are healthy hard corals on the reef and also growing on the side of the ship.

The largest nudibranch in the world was found crawling lazily on the hard coral reef next to the ship. It looks like a meat lover's pizza and weighs in at over four pounds. Nearby is a sunken WWII plane just up the reef east of the ship.

34) Family Beach

Location: Glass Breakwater
Attractions: Heavy coral growth
Depth: 2 to 60 feet
Logistics: Beach or boat dive

Dogleg Reef, known also a Family beach and Hobie beach, is a place where the whole family can enjoy the underwater world. A sparsely covered ledge drops off to about 25 feet of sandy bottom. This ledge can be followed around to the richer growth at Dogleg.

Dogleg is a leisurely dive that allows a diver plenty of bottom time. There are coral nooks and crannies that hide octopi and eels. Wrasses, damsels and parrotfish are common and there are various clownfish colonies scattered throughout. One large concentration of anemones and clownfish is particularly photogenic. It sits in about four feet of water next to an artistic stand of fire coral. The anemones are actually fluorescent red.

There is sunken car here too. It is a Toyota, in case you're curious, but I have never heard the story of its demise.

FaiFai Beach and Tumon Bay
as seen from Two Lover's Cliff

Rota Dive Sites

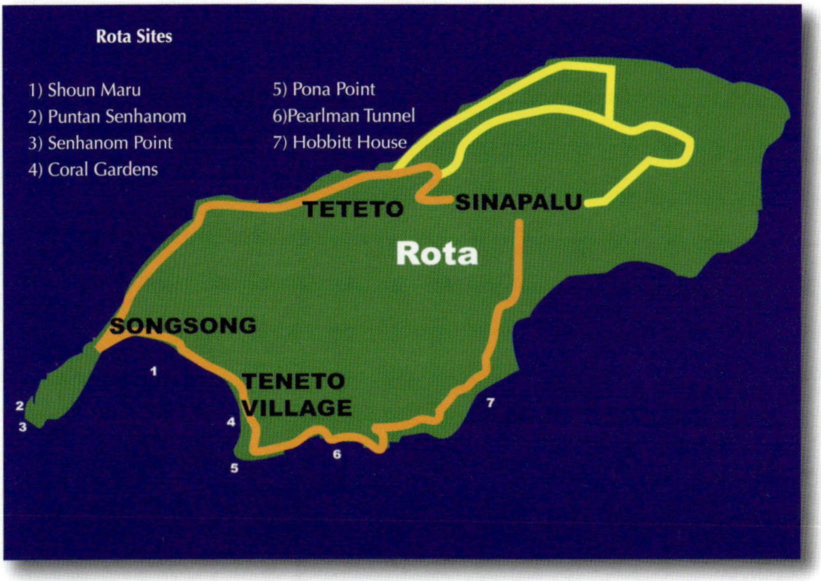

Saipan Dive Sites

Rota's Mochong Beach

Rota's east coast

The Northern Mariana Islands

Known for their clear waters and coolection (short for cool collection) of reefs, caves and war wrecks, Saipan and Rota are favorites of many Asian divers and snorkelers. The climate in the CNMI, or Commonwealth of the Northern Mariana Islands, has been described as one of the most favorable in the world. Hot sunny days and cool nights are the norm.

The isles are the northernmost part of Micronesia, sprawling over a thousand miles in a molten line from north to south in the western Pacific. They start actually with Guam, but it is not politically part of the commonwealth. So rugged Rota is where the CNMI begins and runs north to inhabited and mostly uninhabited outposts. Many of the northernmost Mariana Islands are still active volcanoes. A flight from the capitol of Saipan to Japan will show the smoking calderas of Anatahan, Pagan and Maug in the far north.

Booby in fight

In the south, these geographically quiet islands are alive with marine life and the clearest waters found anywhere. The two most popular islands are Saipan and Rota, where old war wrecks, pelagic congregations and warm waters beckon scuba divers.

The islands themselves offer a rugged beauty with uplifted dragonbacks and plateaus creating a center spine with thick jungles. Cascading waterfalls flow from some of Rota's heights. Saipan is pocked with caves.

Tinian has stunning cliffs that fall to the deep blue sea. People come here to golf, mountain bike, hike and explore World War II battle sites. And, there are some lush botanical gardens here. Beach activities are myriad and the water is warm, so everyone can enjoy the sea.

West coast sunset

Rota, Rugged and Exciting

Just a 20-minute hop by commuter plane opens a whole new world of diving for the scuba buff. Rota, part of the Commonwealth of the Northern Marianas, is a ruggedly beautiful island with a low population density and some exceptionally clear waters like those found in southern Guam. A visiting diver needs a valid passport to enter as Rota is a different political entity from Guam. Virtually all other conditions found on Guam apply. Temperature,

SongSong Village

Shoun Maru

currency, etc. are all the same and Rota has a nice variety of small hotels and local and hotel restaurants for the visitors (and a small casino).

The Northern Marianas island chain extends far north and are "low" coral uplift and volcanic islands with coastlines ranging from rugged rocky cliffs to wide white and black sand beaches. Inland areas are mostly forested with indigenous and introduced species. Some islands are fringed with coral reefs which enclose clear shallow lagoons. Limestone caves and marine grottoes are found on all of the main islands. Many of the northern islands are still geologically active.

Rota has one of the finest seabird sanctuaries in the Pacific and it is easily accessed free of charge. Natural

Seven Screws Wreck

swimming holes, long, untouched sandy beaches, a rugged "Sabana" plateau and thrusting limestone cliffs and deep dripstone filled caves are all parts of the natural attractions. Despite the proximity to Guam, the brown tree snake does not plague the Northern Marianas. Because of this, the islands are blessed with over 40 indigenous and introduced bird species. The lucky visitor may even spot the occasional rare deer. There are also monitor lizards and fruit bats in the more rural areas. A profusion of tropical shrubs, flowers and trees cover all the islands. Hibiscus, Hong Kong orchid, ironwood, banyan, African tulip, papaya, banana, coconut and plumeria trees are everywhere. And the lucky visitor who comes in May and June will witness the spectacular flowering of the brilliant red flame trees that are found on the island.

Under the water, the surrounding coral reefs abound with tropical fish of every description and color, as well as marine turtles and some reef sharks. The surrounding ocean is home to several large species of game fish such as marlin, mahi-mahi, tuna, barracuda, ulua and assorted bottom fish.

Rota has a selection of hard corals on the fringing reefs. Sea fans and lace corals adorn the steep outer dropoffs. Schools of barracuda and jacks can be seen in the blue water. Fascinating caves with shafts of sunlight pouring through are found at relatively shallow depths and there are some WWII remnants, including that of a large freighter.

1) Shoun Maru & Seven Screws
Location: Sasonaya Bay, Rota
Attractions: Shipwrecks & Fish Life
Depth: 25-30 meters

This has been Rota's premier wreck dive for decades and even though

Bottlenose dolphins swim toward the Wedding Cake

Senhanom Cave

the ship is showing some sign of age, she attracts a healthy selection of marine life and her big bow still cuts a pretty profile. The WWII Japanese freighter Shoun Maru is upright and splayed wide open. It was sunk June 23, 1944 by an aerial torpedo. On most days the diver can see the entire 400-foot long wreck from the surface. There's also the Seven Screws wreck. This narrow ship was sunk for sport diving but once plied the rivers of China. It was confiscated at part of a human smuggling bust. The seabed around both wrecks is alive with garden eels. The ships attract whitetips sharks and spadefish.

2) Senhanom Cave
Location: West Wedding Cake
Attractions: Light-filled Cavern
Depth: 30- 80 feet

For divers, the Rota water clarity is astounding. A bad day is 100 feet. And it has a honeycombed base that extends to the sea, opening up a selection of caves, tunnels and crevices that are fun to explore, full of life and simply stunning when dived at the right time of day. One of the more photographed and famous sites in Rota is along the west shoreline at the Wedding Cake Point. Puntan Senhanom, literally translated from Chamorro means The Water Point, is a cavern that is lit through a dual opening by the sun.

The dive entails heading straight for the cliffline, which falls vertically into the sea. The dark opening of a cave becomes apparent and at about 40 or so feet, the cave can be entered. The cavern itself is huge and walls are covered in encrusting sponges. Unlike most caves, this one doesn't get darker with further penetration, it gets lighter. The best time to visit here is varies by season, when the rotating sun streams

Coral Gardens

down through an opening in the cliff and sends shafts of light into the hole. It is possible to swim to the light source and rise through it. Check with local operators to get the exact time of day for the full experience.

Many describe watching the blue dancing shafts of light as a mystical experience. Some Japanese dive shops even bring divers in to sit on the cave floor and quietly meditate.

Once can swim back to the rear where schools of bigeyes and sweepers reside. There is also a place one can actually surface and take off gear to have a look at the other opening that leads to the rough Wedding Cake limestone.

Whitetip sharks like to rest on ledges near the entrance of the cave. On the outside, look for a Napoleon wrasse or an occasional dogtooth tuna to cruise by in the open ocean.

3) Senhanom Point
Location: West Wedding Cake
Attractions: Wall and Boulders
Depth: 30- 130 feet

Clear, blue and deep, the southern end of Rota can be a very cool dive. Huge boulders and a hard slope hold sea fans, golden crinoids and beautiful lace corals.

The big chance for something from the open ocean to swim in here is why many divers do this dive.

Mahi-Mahi, wahoo, reef sharks and even bottlenose dolphin pods may come by in the blue expanse leading to

Rota Swimming Hole

the channel and trench separating Rota from Guam. This point and the deeper water off the oint is a favorite fishing spot so it is even possible yellowfin tuna or feeding whale sharks could breeze by.

This is normally a slow drift dive and you can really select your depth. Look also for resting whitetips sharks along the bottom. They like to relax and have the current push water over their bodies and through their gills.

The waves crash against the boulders and upper reef in some places. As the sun filters through, it can be very surreal and photogenic.

4) Coral Gardens

Location: West Wedding Cake
Attractions: Hard corals & fish
Depth: 10- 50 feet

This dive site was once a popular walk-in dive but now is done mostly by boat. Divers of just about any level as well as snorkelers can have a blast at the aptly-named Coral Gardens. This area has mounds and slopes and hills and valleys of hard corals. Mostly it is cascading castle coral with spires at the top and plating action down below.

This provides lots of habitat for small invertebrates like cowries, Christmas tree worms and even lobsters. To entertain divers, operators sometimes feed the fish so expect to see very friendly double-saddle butterflyfish, threadfin butterflyfish and surgeonfish all hoping for a handout.

Quiet Rota Road

This reef also attracts sea turtles. Look at the deeper depths and out into the sandy plain at the bottom of the reef for the turtles and also for garden eels and peacock flounder that inhabit the sand flats.

Rota also has a few historic WWII remnants nearby in the sand, although much of these small ships were destroyed by a Navy EOD team that was dispatched to get rid of old depth charges.

The upper parts of the reef are great for snorkeling. Lots of fish hide and roam over the nooks and crannies of this amazing patch of hard coral.

The site is normally protected from surge and waves by Pona Point. It has clear water and is easily accessible.

5) Pona Point
Location: Sasonaya Bay SE Tip
Attractions: Sea Fans & Barracuda
Depth: 10- 90 feet

This site is at the eastern end of the Sasonaya Bay and there are three good dive spots in the vicinity.

The most interesting may be where a limestone ridge rises in the current and a wall and overhang full of sea fans highlights the marine life here. Look for snapper and batfish schools. Also, look in the blue for a shoal of blackbar barracuda. You can drift to this spot by starting along the east coast and drifting at 30-50 feet. There is a large sea turtle population here that eats an algae that grows along the reef flats.

One can choose to go deeper and see what is living in the sandy bottom. Pufferfish also like some of the protective undercuts. Starfish with tiny commensal shrimp can be found along the reef as well.

Out at the point the current can get strong so this dive requires a good boat driver and a safety sausage. It is here the sea fans, sea whips, barracuda and batfish schools and pelagics are found.

Pona Point fans and sea whips

6) Pearlman Tunnel
Location: Southeast Cliffline
Attractions: Cavern, fans, sharks
Depth: 80 - 20 feet

Other caves also show a penchant for housing marine life. Pearlman Tunnel is one such site that is home to a couple of whitetip sharks. The cave has an entrance at about 80 feet and runs up a slope to less than 20 feet where it opens up again. The silhouette of the sharks swimming nervously back and forth can be seen as the diver enters the cave.

Normally not aggressive, the sharks will leave while their home is being explored. But they usually don't stray too far, occasionally swimming by on the outer reef to see if it is okay to come back and take a rest stop.

This site and Pona Point nearby have forests of golden gorgonian fans that give off a brilliant hue when the underwater light is shined on them.

7) Hobbit House
Location: Central - east Cliffline near Bird Sanctuary
Attractions: Swim-throughs, jacks
Depth: 50 feet

Near Rota's Bird Sanctuary is an odd formation called the Hobbit House. This huge rock is full of large passages. The ceiling of the House is covered in delicate lace corals and encrusting sponges and tunicates line the walls.

Batfish in blue water

A school of skipjacks has made this site its home. Like the sharks, they will swim nervously from passage to passage and streak a diver in a flash of silver when he or she least expects it.

The setting for all of these caves is the majestic eastern coastline. Rivers flow right down to the sea here and coconut lined groves cover the mountains where the water has run through the jungle.

A certain sites, the boat engines can be cut and waterfalls can be heard gurgling and splashing over the last shelf of rocks before it becomes part of the ocean.

Diving into these haloclines of mixed sea and fresh water can be a little disorienting, like looking at the world with petroleum jelly on your glasses.

Sagua Ghaga Seabird Sanctuary

Birds, especially sea birds, are one of the Rota's claims to fame. Its bird sanctuary on the east coast is set in one of the most scenic of sites in the Pacific. Few places in the Pacific offer the panoramic view of nature that you'll find at the Sagua Ghaga seabird sanctuary, with its layered overlooks and recently refurbished walkways built into a sheer cliffline.

Situated on the edge of a high cliff, this overlook is a loft over the lush green roosts of the red-footed boobies that nest in the trees below. Brown boobies nest in the cliffs, together with brown noddies, white-tailed and red-tailed tropicbirds, and fairy terns. The immense greater frigate bird often soars overhead, and collared kingfishers rattle a noisy call while they roost on the railing. The endangered Mariana crow is not an uncommon visitor here, nor is the Mariana fruit bat.

Along with the ocean-faring birds, nearly all of Rota's forest birds can be seen here. Less frequently you may see or hear a deer, and looking out to sea, you're all but guaranteed to catch a glimpse of a green sea turtle surfacing for a breath of air, and pods of dolphins occasionally swim past.

The sanctuary overlook was completed in October 1992, after a long period of construction, and comprises a series of concrete steps winding down to a railed viewing area along the cliff top. Prior to 1992, hiking to the edge was a bit dicier, leaning over the edge to capture a glimpse of the birds a bit more risky. The concrete overlook creates a safe nature viewing area accessible to everyone. Trees and time hide the ancient latte sites below.

Down below Rota's Bird Sanctuary, the sea crashes into the cliffs.

Undersea Ballet

The islands of Micronesia in the Western Pacific Ocean hold many surprises. In the Northern Mariana island of Rota, is the product of many geologic uplifts, giving the island the look of a wedding cake and creating some amazing undersea complexes.

Complimented by Rota's legendary clear water, the Senhanom Tunnel is one such natural feature. This saltwater vertical chasm is fed by light, creating dancing shafts of blue at certains times of the day. Normally lasting for just a couple of hours, this Mother Nature light show is unrivaled.

The submerged tunnel can become a studio as it opens itself to come creative photography. Here underwater model Elaine Kwok creates an undersea ballet using the rugged cave features and the light from the heavens for a series of images in the palace of Neptune.

Tanapag lagoon & WWII Tank

The Beauty of Saipan

The island of Saipan is the capitol of the Commonwealth of the Northern Mariana Islands (CNMI) and is a quick five-hour trip by jet from Hong Kong and most other Asian airports. From Guam, it is but 55-minute hop by commuter prop jet or 25 minutes by commercial jet.

The PIC hotel on the west coast of Saipan has a large water park, punctuated by a replica of an ancient Manila galleon, a tribute to a gold ship that sunk on the nearby coast. But whether it be treasure or bountiful marine life, Saipan is a place that holds many secrets beneath its sea.

The island is also famous for clear water. Divers are now coming to see a new underwater attraction, schooling eagle rays of off Managaha Island. Managaha is a very good and popular snorkeling site.

Saipan is fun to explore, has a fascinating pre-war background and somewhat grisly wartime period and offers stunning western beaches.

There are some unique dives here. Across the channel, some diving is also done on Tinian, which is best known for having a gambling casino and being the launching isle for the Enola Gay and the dropping of the atomic bomb on Japan in WWII.

Rumor also has it that the famous aviatrix Amelia Earhart was captured after her round-the-world record attempt ended in a plane crash. She supposedly was held in Saipan's

Forbidden Island (Isleta Maigo Luao)

Japanese jail, which is now a tourist attraction. The truth of her demise remains under debate decades later.

Saipan has a great night scene, nice restaurants and a superb sunset.

1) Eagle Ray City
Location: Tanapag Harbor, Saipan
Attractions: Schooling Eagle Rays
Depth: 22-35 feet
Logistics: Boat Dive

In only 22-35 feet of water with bright white sand and blue seas, there is an eagle ray dive in the harbor that is an amazing sight. Anywhere from 5 to 35 rays gather at a couple of current-fed spots in the bay to feed and play in the moving water. The key to this dive is the current.

One must go down and just sit still and wait and the rays may come quite close. Since it is almost all sandy bottom, this can be tricky if the current is strong. Some dive operators have placed a rope in the current area but the rays don't always go where the rope is. A bit of extra weight helps anchor you a bit on this dive.

The beautiful patterns of the snouted eagle rays and their balletic movements are worth holding firm in the currents to snap a few nice shots.

It is here one gets an idea of just how clear the water is. The place resembles a swimming pool and it is easy to get lulled into a sense of serenity as one watches the antics of the rays as they play with each other and with the changing strengths of the currents.

The eagle ray dive is a seasonal event that takes place mostly in spring and summer, but there are also a couple of nice dives on the outer reef that feature the rays.

Spotted eagle rays

2) Tanapag Harbor Wrecks
Location: Tanapag Harbor, Saipan
Attractions: Fish and War Remnants
Depth: 20 to 50 feet
Logistics: Boat dive,

Nearby the ray dive in the harbor are WWII airplanes, ships and remnants complete with whitetip sharks and resident eels.

In all, there are about eight sites a diver or snorkeler could visit here. They include Suehiro Maru, A Japanese submarine chaser, three landing craft, a seaplane, A Japanese float plane, and American plane and a mini-sub.

Sea plane engine & propeller

Tanapag Lagoon

The wartime wrecks are in shallow water clouded with schools of goatfish and snappers. One badly mangled ship is also called the Shoun Maru, similar to that one in Rota, and the CIA in the cold war years used it for target practice. But it is a great artifical reef now that normally features clear water in shallow depths so long overswims and swim-arounds can be made at this site. Aside from the large goatfish schools there are sleeping whitetip sharks under the twisted metal of the ship and the planes and an eagle ray may swim by.

If you are a history buff and have a boat to yourself, your guide can take you to three or four of these wrecks and you won't use up your tank as they are all fairly shallow. The sub chaser sticks partly out of the water but the rest require the help of a guide to find.

There are also some sites outside of Tanapag Lagoon heading right from the mouth that have landing craft (photo Page 102) left over from the war.

WWII Japanese gun

WWII in Saipan

Unlike Guam, which was a United States possession prior to the war, Saipan was part of Japan. But it became an important stepping stone in the U.S. push to end the war.

As it turned out, the Marianas Campaign of World War II was the most decisive battle of the Pacific Theater. U.S. Forces were able to cut off vital Japanese supply and communication lines, and American B-29 bombers moved within range of the Japanese homeland. The end of the war with Japan followed 14 months later.

The initial move to take Saipan started at 0840 on June 15, 1944. It was at that time initial waves of the 2nd and 4th U.S. Marine Divisions stormed onto a narrow beachhead on Saipan. The enemy guns were ranged-in on the beaches and shells rained down. Many died in the exchange.

Marine units, supported by Naval and Army Air Corps bombardment, and joined by the U.S. Army's 27th Infantry Division, waged savage warfare. For most of the soldiers, seamen, and airmen it was yet another invasion. For many it would be their last. For the world it was the beginning of the end of the Pacific War. It took nearly a month but Saipan was declared secured on July 9th.

Today one can visit the American Memorial Park which honors the American and Marianas people who gave their lives during World War II. The park is centrally located along the western shoreline of Saipan, adjacent to downtown Garapan.

Over 5,000 names are inscribed on a memorial which was dedicated during the 50th anniversary of the Invasion of Saipan. It features beaches, sports fields, picnic sites, boat marinas, playgrounds, walkways, and a 30-acre wetland and mangrove forest.

Managaha Island

3) Managaha Island
Location: Tanapag Harbor, Saipan
Attractions: Fish and War Remnants
Depth: 10 to 30 feet
Logistics: Shore Dive, Boat dive or snorkel

One of Saipan's most popular day trips is a visit to Managaha Island. Beautiful shallow coral gardens can be found off the shores here. A snorkel is all you really need to enjoy feeding the fish and swim in the usually warm and clear waters.

One side of the island has the remnants of some WWII landing craft and one side is beautiful sandy beaches. Most snorkelers will opt for the coral gardens which hold clear waters and a variety of hard corals, well-fed fish. One can venture offshore or take a two-minute boat trip to some popular coral gardens that always seem to get rave reviews. Underwater photographers can dive here and spend lots of time taking fish photos.

The island is fun too. It is touristy, but local families often go there so there is a good chance to mingle with the Saipanese. A walk around Managaha usually takes no more than 15-minutes and there is a t WWII gun emplacement with a Japanese cannon. There is also a memorial to a revered Carolinian chief.

After snorkeling stop at the snack bar for some cool ice cream.

4) Wing Beach
Location: West central Saipan Coast
Attractions: Arch and Wall
Depth: 30 to 90 feet
Logistics: Boat Dive

This dive can be done from shore going through a cut at the north end of the beach but it is easier and, if there is any surf at all, safer to go by boat.

The attraction is a beautiful coral arch covered in sponges and delicate lace corals. This site has the possibility of delivering pelagic sea life and there is also a big coral canyon to explore.

Dive with the cliffline on the right on the way to the arch and you can see the surf crashing overhead. Small sponges, corals and sea whips grow along this sloping wall. Lionfish like the crannies in the reef here.

5) Banzai Cliff
Location: West central Saipan Coast
Attractions: Open Ocean
Depth: 30 to 130 feet
Logistics: Boat Dive

Banzai Cliff is a dive that can only be done when it is calm. You can visit the site by car and look down at the big rocks and crashing waves. Usually, you'll see a sea turtle swimming in the blue below.

Dive this site in the calm months by boat and be on the lookout for reef sharks, dolphin schools, sea turtles, big marble rays and the occasional manta and a beautiful wall covered in lace corals, crinoids and some sea fans.

The waves will probably still be crashing overhead even when it is calm. There are also nice coral formations around this open ocean site as well as numerous sea anemones.

Go with a good guide and boat man as this place can be currenty and you may have to go with the flow.

Banzai Cliff

Lace coral below Banzai Cliff

6) The Grotto
Location: Before Bird Island
Attractions: Cavern of Marine Life
Depth: 35-100 feet
Logistics: Beach Dive down stairs

The Grotto, probably Saipan's most famous novelty dive, requires a bit of a hike up and down a long flight of steps to march down (tank, weights and all). But its is worth the effort. Here a gaping cave greets divers. High, exposed overhead stalactites of this partially collapsed cave still drip.

The diver steps off a big boulder and a new world opens below. Three windows to the sea open are caste in a blue hue that has to be seen to believed.

Outside, big boulders hold fish life large and small, golden sea fans and even an occasional manta ray will swim by. Always do this dive with an experienced guide. It is extremely easy to get lost in the big boulders and not find your way back to the Grotto windows. If you have to surface outside, it is sheer cliffs. Not a good alternative.

Experienced Grotto divers swear by going early in the morning to both beat the crowds, have nice, soft light and see the most marine life. A good morning high tide usually guarantees clear water as well, increasing visibility outside.

The walls of the cave have some beautiful encrusting sponges as well. For the photographer using a wide angle lens, this dive opens all sorts of possibilities depending on the light at the time of day you dive.

Save some energy as the hike back up the stairs with weights and wet gear is no simple task. But the Grotto is so cool, you'll want to go again. I have one friend who made three dives in one day and she would have gone a fourth time if it wasn't getting dark. Cool dive site.

WWII US landing craft

Bird Island

7) Dimple
Location: West central Saipan Coast
Attractions: Lots o' Fish
Depth: 30 to 100 feet
Logistics: Boat Dive

This Saipan seamount on the island's west side not too far down the coast from the harbor is a great place to watch fish, especially pyramid butterflyfish.

The pyramids engulf divers when fish food is brought out. It is a great place for video with swirling colors. Coral here is very healthy and the dive can be done anywhere from 30 to 120 feet, making it suitable for all levels. The hard coral here is very nice.

8) Obyan Beach
Location: Southern Saipan
Attractions: Fish and Critters
Depth: 15-60 feet
Logistic: Beach or boat dive

This is a favorite walk-in dive for many Saipan resident divers and this bay and dive site holds lots of small critters like mantis shrimp for divers to see and photographers to try to capture.

The entry is a sandy walk-in. Look for turtles to gather and feed on sponges and encrusting growth in the area. Green sea turtles are seen frequently on this dive. On the sea floor, look for peacock flounder skittering across the bottom and garden eels in the deeper

Bubble tip sea anemone

reaches of the dive.

The rocks here provide good habitat for hunting octopus. Lizardfish sit quietly perched waiting patiently in ambush for a meal to swim by.

The site has a nice selection of photogenic sea anemones with one-stripe clownfish and Peterson shrimp in some species. Others are home to tomato clownfish and porcelain crabs.

Take time to look under the coral outcrops for lionfish and sleeping sharks. The beach is favorite to have a picnic lunch. There is a large WWII concrete bunker here and remains of latte stones said to date to 1500 BC.

Best of the Rest - Tinian

Blue Grotto – Across the channel at Tinian is a similar dive to the Saipan Grotto but the entry is much easier (as is the exit and there's no hike back up a hill). This open cave is entered from the sea. Here divers can admire the light shafts and see lionfish and other tropicals inside the cave. Exit is done through one of three open arches to the sea. Big and blue, this is one of the favorite Tinian novelty dives.

Banzai Cliff memorial

Pyramid butterflyfish at Dimple

The islands of the CNMI are a great getaway for the diving enthusiast. Tinian, across a channel from Saipan, also offers some cool dives and there is talk of a live aboard soon to travel to the northern islands. Check out these islands for a great commune with Nature.

For more information on Rota, Saipan, Tinian and the Northern Mariana Islands, see the website: **http://www.visit-marianas.com**

Caring for Our Ocean

Out of sight above the water is not necessarily out of mind down below. In some places on Guam where currents carry discarded items to eddy areas, you can see debris from the land gather. At this spot pictured above in Agat Bay, the results of what might be many weeks fishing have accumulated to litter the sea floor.

The ocean environment is growing more fragile seemingly daily. Nuclear spills in Japan, oil gushing from the Gulf of Mexico, El Nino bleaching reefs in Malaysia and Indonesia... the list seems endless. Man is the responsible entity for the state of our oceans today and only man can reverse that trend.

If you are just one diver, you can pitch in by action and example. Guam has a number of annual sponsored beach and reef clean-ups. These are normally volunteer actions that are fun and a constructive way to spend time helping nurse Mother Ocean back to health.

Read about our seas and know the small things you can do while diving. Try not to touch the corals. Watch your fins so they don't break corals or kick sand on them. Insist on safe anchoring when you dive with an operator or dive on a friend's boat.

And lead by example. Practice what you preach about ocean health and you will see others follow your lead.

The world of the reef is an amazing place. We all need to work together to see it passed on to the next generation.

Know Your Limits

We would like to inject just a word of caution about diving the reefs in and around Guam and the Mariana Islands. For the most part, divers should not experience the ripping currents that often confront a diver in the popular dive hotspots like The Philippines or Indonesia.

Even in this region, currents in Palau and Yap's channels can be stronger and more extreme. Still, a good safety sausage is a must when diving the reefs here. Currents can come up, sudden swells can roll in and a diver may also, for whatever reason, find him or herself in trouble and need to signal the boat or someone on shore.

Better to be safe than sorry and carry one of these signaling devices at all times.

Also, since the water here is so clear, you may not think you are diving as deep as you really are. Always use a computer in the Marianas and be conservative.

Finally, all of the islands, especially Guam and Saipan, offer some great beach dives. But remember that the surf here breaks on hard coral reef and then flows into shallow reef flats. All that water has to come in and then escape somewhere. Depending on the size of the surf, this can make currents in the usual entry and exit cuts treacherously strong. And the reef break can really pound an unsuspecting diver.

Only go over the reef for shore dives when it is very calm.

Tumon Bay, Guam